Remembering **Ruthie**

The Life of Ruth McDowell Kinnard

Remembrances of her friends and family

Cold Tree Press
Nashville, Tennessee

Library of Congress Control Number: 2006924710

Published by Cold Tree Press
Nashville, Tennessee
www.coldtreepress.com

Dedication

*In loving memory of
Ruth McDowell Kinnard*

Table of Contents

Family

Introduction

Judith Kinnard Cabot
Ruth's Daughter

The idea for this book came on the night of the wake, May 17th, 2001. The wounds were still raw when our older daughter, Heath, gave me this poem. A glorious Sunday visit had ended, only days later, in death. And I wanted to grasp at all the memories I could to keep from letting go.

MOTHER'S DAY
Heath Cabot

Heaven fell to
   Earth
      Arrived a gentle wind
        To find herself
          Here.
—From the Book of Changes

My mother's mother is dying today
This sunny Sunday in early May
In the bruised arms of old Natchez Way

In this, my wet and blooming South
The breath is burning her open mouth

And shriveling her mother tongue
In this, my mother land

Where the dogwoods are knots of clotted pink
And thistles pierce the fields

How are we to begin
her birth her death?
She arrived one day a gentle wind
a small breath.
A child squeals across the hall, with her mother, in the bathroom
and I get up to close the quiet door
to this dying room
where the small persistent breath is all
and the pure insistent pulse falls.

Do not disturb us.
Child, your breath is hard and wild with newness.
Let us breathe softly with her awhile
for she will die – and soon.

Mother, your mother is dying today
and I don't know what to say
But Mama, I am so sad.
As her small breath falls to slow groans
And her cheeks draw taut and horrible over the bones
Mama, you are not alone.

How are we to end
her birth, her death,
this gentle wind,
this small breath?

The spirit of a child is floating above the fields
The child loves her mother
who has wells in her wounded eyes and cheeks.
The fields are pierced with thistles
breaking the blue grass with speared leaves.

ii

She walks the fields,
the child presses her swelling breast.
Her welling wounds will never heal,
but her tears are blessed.

Things got in the way. And I thought I had lost my chance. But Tandy, our cousin and a life long friend, persisted. And his enthusiasm is the primary reason for the book you hold in your hand. Equally important is the help provided by my husband, Chris Cabot, and his former legal assistant and our dear friend, Laura Morgan, who prepared much of the text from her new home on the west coast of Ireland.

Perhaps we have all benefited, as we often do, with the passage of time. To remember now, for me at least, brings more comfort and less pain. More smiles are possible, though often through rivulets of tears.

I am so grateful for the outpouring of response from the contributors. I know how difficult this project may have been. I think Bert Phillips put it best: "Perhaps the reason it was so hard for me to write a commemoration for Ruth (and I'll bet this was true for many of us) was that, although she never officially became a priest, Ruth was a confidante and a person to whom it felt natural for me to confess. Our friendship felt private."

I felt an even greater hesitation. You are her friends, even though many of you met her through a friendship with me. I am the interloper, inserting myself into the middle of that very private relationship. I hope you will feel, as I do, that this sharing of intimacy is worth the effort. We may, together through our disparate lenses, project a faithful image for those who will come after and might find guideposts here for a life well lived and loved.

Thank you all.

— *The Lilacs*
Beverly Farms, Massachusetts
January, 2006

Madeline Blue
Ruth's Sister

When asked to recall memories of a person dear to you, you need the help of the Holy Spirit because there are so many wonderful memories. What to tell? Ruth and I were born and lived until Ruth was five and I was ten years old on a 2,000 acre cotton plantation in South Alabama, near Camden.

Liberty Hall was built by our great grandfather for his bride, and Liberty Hall has been in the family all these years, now owned by a cousin of ours. And it is just as beautiful now as it was when it was built.

My mother was left a widow when she was very young, 27 years old. Our father, Angus McDowell, died when he was 37 years old in the flu epidemic years ago. My mother, knowing that she could not operate and manage a 2,000 acre plantation, and having family in Montgomery, Alabama, sold the plantation, and we moved to Montgomery. Our growing up years and schooling were in Montgomery; however we have wonderful memories of this home in Camden.

Ruth's character and outlook on life, I believe, was formed by the many, many loving family members and interesting people she knew during her growing up years. I do believe that a person's outlook and character are definitely formed by associates all during one's life.

Ruth was a happy, caring, joyous child growing up, and the same as a teenager, in high school and college, always thinking about other people. This characteristic she carried throughout her life.

Ruth was a devout Christian. She didn't talk her religion. She lived it. Ruth took other people's cares and lives so much to herself that many times I felt she burdened herself. However, that was what she wanted to do and she relied on the Holy Spirit to help her accept the thoughts and concerns of other people.

I have seen Ruth sit for hours and listen to someone's concerns and then offer to try and help in any way she could.

Ruth's idea for other people was for them to reach their best

potential, and she did everything she could to set the example and to offer assistance in this happening. Now it was not only to one person or one family, but it was to everyone who needed her.

I can remember so vividly Ruth's running into the kitchen when cook was making cookies and getting a plate and running across the street, taking them to the old caretaker at the First Baptist Church and sitting on the brick wall and talking to him. That was not a one time affair. She always remembered him and other people in the same manner.

Ruth was a very intelligent person. This was a gift from God, of course. However, Ruth did her best. She studied. She worked at whatever she was doing, and did her best in every school activity or work.

Now when Ruth was very young, about in the third grade, she brought her report card home once, and she didn't get a very high mark in deportment. Of course, our mother went to the school and talked to the teacher. And the teacher said, "Oh that's not because Ruth misbehaved. It's just that Ruth always knows the answer to any question I am asking and puts up her hand and is very anxious to answer the question. However, the other children sometimes need a little more time to think about it, and so I have to discourage Ruth." We all had a big laugh over that. Ruth always did her best in every activity she undertook.

Now she was a very popular person. People enjoyed her company. She was very talented. She could sing and recite. So she had a very active life.

She worked a year or two for her Tri Delta Sorority after finishing the University of Alabama, and later she was the national president. World War II came along about that time, and things were very different all over the country.

During that time Ruth met in Montgomery, Claiborne Kinnard from Franklin, Tennessee, who was at the Air Force base in Montgomery. They grew to love each other and married just before Claiborne's fighter group was sent to England.

Now during those years, it was a difficult time because you never knew how the War was going, especially for the fighter pilots.

My husband was in the service also. And I went to Alabama to be with her when her oldest child was born.

It was just at the time when you would read in the paper that 25 fighter pilots went out and ten were lost. And you never knew if that would be your family member. So it was a difficult time. But we all lived through it. Claiborne came home after making quite a record for himself. And they established their home in Franklin, Tennessee. Ruth had two other children, two sons.

Now Ruth continued her way of life when she went to Franklin which meant her interest in other people, her interest in the town, interest in anything that could better the town. And she was particularly active in St. Paul's Episcopal Church.

When Claiborne died, he had a long illness, and it was very hard for Ruth and the family. Ruth, wondering what she was going to do, decided to go to law school. And when I asked her why she was undertaking that now, she said, "I want to have something important to get up for every morning. I don't want to spend all my time playing bridge and going to luncheons," which she enjoyed with friends. She didn't want that to be her total outlook.

And as a lawyer and bankruptcy judge and in private practice, she continued in her way of life. I believe Ruth received an award from the Nashville Bar Association, an award for giving the most pro bono services. But her life always was with the same values that she gave her life to the causes that she felt were what God would have her do.

When I think back on the things she accomplished, I am reminded of what a lady told me once. When someone was saying some of the things that I had done, she said, "I don't want to hear about that. All I want to know is does she know Jesus."

Now in answer to that question, I certainly can say that Ruth knew her Lord and Savior, and that was the real life she followed. And I think that was a tremendous tribute to her.

Madeline McDowell Blue

Tandy Rice
Longtime Friend and Confidant

GENTLE READER: Abandon, if you can, the rather myopic notion that our lady was defined by robes, gavels, legaleze, the courtrooms, haughtiness of the judiciary and other such trappings. Trust me. I, Tandy C. Rice Jr., am here today to give sworn testimony to another dimension of Her Honor. One that you may not even know about, but one that is indelibly tattooed on my psyche til the end of time.

And that is...that..."RUTHIE WAS A BABE!!"

Take it from these lips, these two eyes and these trembling hands as I try to recount for you an incident of my youth which both terrified and taunted me, and forever redefined my understanding of my small world. It definitely turned my 9-year-old head.

As a third or fourth grader, my first "coming together" with Ruth Kinnard was clouded by the sights and sounds of long, lazy summers at Willow Plunge and all the nuances that came into play as a young boy came eye-to-eye with the most beautiful woman he'd ever seen and literally fell forever in love with her in all her glory. It's important that I tell you of her Grace Kelly looks, her style and the statuesque and stunning, regal way she carried herself.

I can still smell the Coppertone suntan oil, Viceroy cigarettes, willow trees, chlorinated water, hand-patted hamburgers and freshly made chess pies. Add to that the sounds of Vaughn Monroe, the Ink Spots and Patty Page, and it really becomes heady stuff.

And for the final capper, her arrival on the scene in the town's only Cadillac followed by her bigger-than-life husband's similar arrival in the town's only Jaguar and HIS good looks that made every man around want to crawl under a nearby rock...and you have the magic mix of factors that are re-awakened in me when I summon up memories of the Ruthie I knew and worshiped from that time until we said goodbye to her privately and quietly at the graveside many years later.

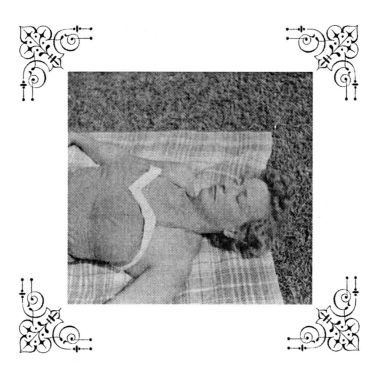

If you will allow me this indulgence, I think it's important for so many folk who became her friends in mid-life to know that there was a distinct side of her that didn't wear a robe or ponder the law. I loved that dimension also. But there was an "early Ruth" in a bathing suit that stopped the crowds on Willow Plunge's hillside and literally defined class, beauty and style for this little boy who was to follow her through our mutual lives with total respect, love and undying adoration even to this day.

I was working my first job as a "maintenance man" at Willow Plunge Swimming Pool. My job was to rake and remove cut grass, pick up paper and other such stuff. For this, I received no pay but got to swim free. This seemed like a good deal to me at the time.

Willow Plunge was a shimmering diamond, the ultimate pleasure spa and one of the most popular recreational spots in Tennessee. It was a huge, huge business success and the Kinnards owned it lock, stock and barrel. They were coining money. And I was picking up trash. We were both happy.

Always crowded in those hot days before air conditioning was everywhere, the boisterous place smelled of suntan oil, chlorine, June bugs and green grass clipped daily by young lads like me. Visually, it was a mind-boggling sight to behold.

"Tandy. Would you help me just a moment?" said this uniquely theatrical voice. I turned and saw a vision from heaven, a combination Grace Kelly and Lauren Bacall with a 100 gold bracelets on her arm and huge sunglasses that spelled high drama.

It was Mrs. Kinnard herself, THE BOSS, in all her glorious, breathtaking, young womanhood.

GULP!! "Yes Maam!!"

"Will you please put some Coppertone on my back and shoulders?"

GULP!! "Yes Maam!!"

I dutifully set out to earn my pay and thought I'd died and gone to heaven. I didn't want the anointing to ever end. Then came: "Will you please put some on the back of my legs?"

GULP!! "Yes Maam!!"

My own legs turned to rubber and it was glorious beyond words. She was the most beautiful thing these young eyes had ever beheld. And when she spoke, there was a lilt and drama to the way she whispered and rolled her words that just made me want to die. I think you know what I mean.

I won't say I became a man that day. But I will say that the passage made me realize, for the first time, that there was "life" outside and beyond my own mama's apron strings.

Right then and there before God and everybody, I fell madly in love with Ruth Kinnard, "The Babe" in the red Catalina bathing suit. I'm still there in love with her today, hopelessly and forever. I just wanted to tell you about this dimension of her great life, since you might have missed out on it. Beats the heck out of a black robe doesn't it?

I hope you get the picture!

Forever yours, Ruthie....

John Beasley

She had grown up in Alabama, and when she came to Franklin in 1946 it was with youth and intelligence and above all else, an indescribable style. Slotted half-way between my parents' age and my own, she was something of an icon to my friends and me. She had married the scion of old Williamson County gentry, and she brought light and laughter to a family which had not experienced a lot of either. Her husband had been a fighter ace in World War II, operating out of British airdromes with far-away and romantic names like Martlesham Heath, Steeple Morden and Saffron Walden, and through her life the homes she lived in bore these names. The tiny old Episcopal parish in our little town could not have had more than forty ancient souls, but St. Paul's became her church. And when, at first, she took her two small children there on Sunday, the attendance rose by about the same margin that the average age fell. She drove fine American cars, and she drove them skillfully. She was blond and beautiful, but she broke that stereotype by being always inquiring and deeply literate.

At war's end, her husband came home to become a successful businessman and something of an inventor. She did what women did in those days, making a home, making the place for him and her children, adding a civility and a verve to our town which differed from that which others brought to it.

People were drawn to her (not always, since north poles of opposing magnets cannot attract), and she talked to them about things in which they were interested. She was discriminating, but she generally found in people some common ground upon which to converse. In the late 50's when I came back from the Navy to marry, she was firmly established in our town.

As a young lawyer, I volunteered with her on a couple of the town's civic projects and came quickly to appreciate her fine qualities of wisdom and wit, as well as the sparkle of a good conversation. I had "found" the Episcopal Church during my Navy days, and as

xii

Allison had been raised in that Church, it was natural for us to join the little one in Franklin. Ruth conducted the confirmation class (from her I learned that "narthex" is what others call "vestibule") and she taught that class year after year. There is no telling how many entered St. Paul's and the Anglican Communion through her door.

Allison's mother and mine died young, leaving our two children grandmotherless. A devoted Ruth was our son's Godmother and our daughter's grandmother, and so much more. Her children were our children's valuable near-kin, and any one of the countless trips to Mama Ruth's was better than Disneyland.

In 1966 her husband was taken from her by a cancer in his brain. There was enough time for her to walk through his latest invention with him, writing down the processes as he described them to her. And then he was gone, leaving an unfillable gap in her life and in the lives of his children. She was forty-seven years old at the time, and her third child, Jon, was only twelve. After a suitable period, she gathered herself and entered Vanderbilt Law School. It was daring and heroic, for the difficulty of the regimen was beyond what she had anticipated. But she did it well and soon the entire law class was her age and she was theirs. Sometime later she told me, "I've always read in the Bible that the Lord giveth and the Lord taketh away. I am now also persuaded that the Lord taketh and the Lord giveth."

Over the next many years, Allison and I were perhaps as close to Ruth as people get. We watched her children and grandchildren grow, and we watched her great style continue, always without ostentation. A black tie party at Martlesham Heath, with Mary Taylor whipping up the goodies and Mr. Charlie in his starched white coat before a huge silver punchbowl full of ice, was always an occasion to cherish and remember. A casually written note from her – Allison kept everything she ever wrote to us – invariably contained some little piece of treasure. I worked for a spell with Ruth at the Commerce Union Bank, before she became a Federal Referee in Bankruptcy and then a practicing attorney in Nashville.

Until the end of her life, she would be most often seen in a becoming black dress with a huge gold Cross on a chain around her neck. Sometimes the Cross would be empty; sometimes a Star of David would be superimposed on it. I called her "The Bishop of Franklin," but her wearing of those signs was never an affectation. In the latter third of her life she was destined to experience intense pain of every sort – relentless physical pain in her back, the economic pain of crippling financial reverses, emotional pain in the death of a beautiful grandson, even the bitter pain of rejection. Job was no more sorely afflicted, and Ruth struggled in her faith. But neither she nor the God in whom she believed would turn the other loose, and Sundays found her in her customary place at St. Paul's, on her knees as long as she could kneel. Tandy Rice and I read at her memorial service when that time finally came, and she was released from a worn and broken body.

For us, Ruth is as present and real today as she ever was, a knowing smile, a throaty laugh, a cigarette between her fingers, her eyes on yours as though there were no one else in the world. Perhaps a bit more ethereal today, but barely more than when you saw her last at a party, or heard her voice on the phone, or walked in on her listening to Frank Sinatra with a Scotch in her hand. We loved her. We always will.

Friends

Jennie Adams

Ruth...A coveted friend.

Ruth...As colorful and elegant as the stained glass windows in her beloved church.

Ruth...An amazing paradox of the old aristocratic South and a modern feminist. While at the same time, so integrated and congruent.

We belonged to a group in Nashville for ten years known as the "Over the Hill Gang." Its purpose was to offer pro bono assistance to those in pursuit of a calling and/or experiencing a choice point or crisis of change in their life.

It was a "Council of Elders" composed of eight retired professionals representing education, clergy, psychiatry, social work, business and psychology. Ruth offered legal and down to earth wisdom. She was invaluable and irreplaceable. When she had to resign because of immense pain, she left a void.

Ruth was an "amphibian," as she seemed to travel effortlessly across classifications and societal boundaries.

To wit, one time we shared a ride to a birthday party of a mutual friend. The guests, some thirty attractive, bright, successful, professional women, were lesbian in sexual orientation and openly comfortable in themselves. Most were total strangers to Ruth. Nonetheless, she drew a captive audience seemingly the entire evening, sharing multiple topics including her career as a pioneering legal professional and judge. On the ride back home she talked of her new acquaintances with great interest, curiosity and admiration.

Several days later, a note from Ruthie arrived in the mail. It simply said, "Jennie – Thank You for broadening my horizons. Love

Ruth." I like to think that she continues to enjoy unlimited horizons. I often think of her when the chimes of the downtown Methodist Church float over our neighborhood. I remember how they brought real pleasure and comfort to her. And her spirit is entwined with the music.

Jennie Adams

Danny Anderson

In my eyes, Ruth Kinnard was the epitome of a true friend – compassionate, thoughtful and giving. She embraced my family with a selfless kindness that endears her to us to this very day. As a friend, we shared the good and bad, happy and sad – as a mentor she shared her infinite wisdom and gave us thoughtful and heartfelt guidance.

I often reflect back to the time when Ruthie lived in her stunning loft apartment above our store "D-Roy Entertains" on 4th Avenue. When we were open she never failed to drop in to check on us and our young son, Reid, whom she always showered with affection. She was a steadfast source of comfort and support when we announced that we were closing the store we so loved after 12 years.

I miss Ruthie's notes – she was a true master of communication – always writing to say "Thank You," "Congratulations" or "Good Luck." I treasured her notes even though I had to have my wife, Teresa, translate her handwriting most of the time. She helped me realize just how important it is to stay in touch with those that mean so much.

One of my greatest regrets is not following through with plans to coordinate a Black Tie dinner to honor Ruthie and her dear friend, Sue Berry, for their many contributions to our community. Time constraints kept me from following through with my "good intentions." I guess we think our heroes will live forever – unfortunately, they don't. But she will live forever in my heart.

It was so ironic that Ruthie joined her heavenly father on the very day that the Heritage Foundation honored Ruthie and Sue at their annual meeting for their dedication and support to the community they so loved. I truly miss them both.

For the Anderson family, Ruthie's star shines as bright as that big shiny gold cross that she always wore. Our lives have been blessed by her friendship and enriched by her example – she was a true friend.

Danny Anderson

Betty Jane Barringer

Most of my memories of Ruth Kinnard center around the time I was growing up in Franklin, the 40's, 50's and early 60's. After that time I lived in Memphis and my main contact with her and her activities was through my parents or the newspaper. She had a whole new life after I left town! Wish I had been around "Judge Kinnard" as much as I was around "Miz Kinnard."

Visiting the Kinnards was always a treat. First, they had a *new* house built all on one story. Then they moved to Martlesham Heath – the first house I had ever known that had a name – I can still see the United States map on the wall in the den. Usually when we visited, there were more than one of us Guffees present, yet Ruth was able to maintain her equilibrium and calm manner no matter how many of us were yelling as we ran through the house. To me, Ruth was the embodiment of glamour, sophistication, charm, and gentility, as she was to most of the young girls who knew her. We also loved the fact that she *hadn't* gone to Vanderbilt and she *wasn't* a Theta; Alabama and Tri Delta sounded different, exotic, and somehow more attractive. It was always exciting to be at Ruth's house and overhear her talking – LONG DISTANCE – to a fellow Tri Delt. And she sometimes traveled alone to places like New York or Dallas for meetings – pretty heady stuff for a Franklin youngster! Additionally, Ruth was a Phi Beta Kappa – an achievement impressive even to a teenager! We wanted to be just like her!

Ruth's handwriting was certainly distinctive – not always readable, but distinctive. We loved her voice, her curly hair, even the fact that she smoked. She made everyone feel special, children as well as adults. She was a non-judgmental listener, one in whom you could confide knowing she would never betray your trust. She loved people of all ages, and we knew it. Her generosity, her warmth, and her hospitality were legendary. She held the keys to our favorite summer haunt, Willow Plunge, and on very special occasions, she would let us swim FREE.

Ruth Kinnard was a giver, not a taker. She loved her family, her church, and her fellow man. She was kind. She had a wonderful sense of humor. She was a hard worker. She shared her time and her talents with no expectation of their being returned. But far and away the best gift Ruth and Clay Kinnard ever gave me was their daughter, Judy. A life-long friend, Judy and I have seen too little of each other since we both left Franklin. But, when we do get together, it's as if we were, once again, girls sitting at the soda fountain at the Corner Drug Store having a coke float. Thank you, Ruth, for the example you set for so many of us, and for your three wonderful children. We love and miss you.

Betty Jane Barringer

Vicki Bartholomew

Longtime Friend and Admirer

Sam met Ruth Kinnard in his first year of Law School (1970) and soon an invitation came for an evening at Martlesham Heath. Ruth met us near Franklin and we followed her home down the tree-lined drive that really took our breaths away. Everything about the evening was incredible. She invited us into the kitchen while she prepared dinner, the fireplaces were blazing, the antiques, the memorabilia, the coffee and conversation are still stamped in my mind. Ruth told us about her family and spoke gently and fondly of her beloved Claiborne. I remember one particular thing she said, "Vicki, I was raised to please a man…when there was no man around, I had great difficulty and decided I had to be able enough to go back to school and do something else." Ruth was the essence of gracious southern hospitality and a woman of incredible courage. I loved her from that first meeting which was the first of many…many of those times at Martlesham Heath.

In the summer of 1976, Sam and I drove to Ruth's home for an afternoon by her pool as we awaited the birth of our second child. My labor started with great fanfare in her back yard, and the event became another memory in our friendship as she took control, calmed all of us and called the doctor as we sped toward the hospital.

In 1976, I had an amazing spiritual transformation when one of my friends prayed with me to ask Jesus to be my Lord and Savior. I had always known Ruth to be a very spiritual person but had stayed away from conversations with her about that area of her life…maybe I had envied her peace and quiet assurance of her faith but before that point, I wanted nothing to do with it! When I opened up to her about what had happened to me, she embraced me long and hard and with tears in her eyes said... "Oh, how fortunate you are...how I wish I had known Jesus at such a young age." At the time, I did not understand much, but now I do understand. Ruth accepted Christ when she was fifty-five, and much heartache had already come her way.

Ruth and I talked often about the Lord...in fact, that was almost all we talked about after that time. I cherished her wise counsel and her strength to stay the course. I marveled at her commitment to be in prayer every morning at 5:30 no matter how much lay ahead of her for the day. She was so happy to share how the Lord had blessed her and was her reason for living. As time went on, she remained an incredible, wonderful friend. She worked with my husband, and we saw each other both at work-related events and socially. Always, our friendship was knit together by knowing how powerfully the Lord had intervened for both of us. We prayed together and for each other. This was a woman who lived her faith and to whom the reality of heaven was very clear.

The last time I saw Ruth was in the rehab center in Nashville a few months before she died. I spoke to her after that only one time. Ruth was, as always, more interested in me and my family that in her own dire situation and was as sweet and smiling as always even though I knew she felt just terrible. We had some prayer time, and then she said something that I must say in this writing. "Vicki, I want all of my family to know Jesus...if you get a chance, Vicki...tell them."

Ruth Kinnard...simply, a woman who loved Jesus and was His extraordinary ambassador to everyone she met. I miss her deeply.

Vicki Bartholomew

Sam Bartholomew

Longtime Friend and Law Partner

Ruth Kinnard was the essence of gifted balance between a beautiful wife and mother, and a professional barrister and counselor. She was a warm, giving, and understanding friend. She always had time for whoever might seek her counsel, unlike most frenetic lawyers. This attitude carried over in her work as the first-ever female Federal Bankruptcy Judge in Tennessee as she became a role model for female judges and professionals.

I never knew anyone who did not love Ruth. I often thought she seemed as though she understood more than the rest of us by valuing personal relationships and allowing those relationships to trump greed and power. Her life would make a great book about what is good and true in life. I have never known anyone like Ruth who could be productive in the market place with a genuine love of people and be a "time giver" to hundreds of friends and acquaintances. She made time stand still when you were with her.

Her Christ-like attitude and golden rule demeanor in counseling had a huge impact on me and countless others. We miss her and look forward to joining her in heaven above!!

Sam Bartholomew

Allison Beasley

The first time I saw Ruth Kinnard was at the Tri Delta house at Vanderbilt when I was a sophomore, and she was the national president of the sorority. I don't remember why she was there to speak to us, but I do remember her impact. She wore a slim black suit and lit a cigarette – in a holder! She settled herself on the sofa, and we sank to the floor around her. Katherine Hepburn would have been less mesmerizing. I can't recall what she said, but I remember well the blond curly hair and the low seductive voice. I wanted to be like her.

It was more than six years before I saw her again, this time when I had moved to Franklin as a newlywed. And there she was, organizing interesting groups and immediately making me a part.

In time she gave us the gift of being our son's Godmother, and soon after, our first puppy – Irma La Douce, a small black poodle. When we had been married ten years, she gave us our first black-tie dinner party at the Heath.

It was the style of the woman – her chic dress, her husky voice, her use of each person's name when she addressed him, her good gold jewelry, her house filled with old silver and fresh roses – that made me follow along, her devoted acolyte. I wanted to be like her.

She was always reading an interesting book and would often come into our living room with a quote from James Agee. She was greatly taken with his letters to Father Flye.

There wasn't a man alive she couldn't charm. At a birthday party we gave for her when she turned seventy-five, a young lawyer there confided in me "I've always found her sexy."

Ruth was like Cleopatra – age could not "wither her, nor custom stale her infinite variety." As her life took its downturns, she held the course, never complaining and always responding with unflinching courage and strength. She seemed to have an endless energy, and she lived fully every minute. During one period she drove each morning to a 6 AM healing service at St. Bartholomew's, then downtown to a full day of law practice before returning home, perhaps to entertain friends for cocktails. She didn't wear out 'til the very end. To me, she was sister, mother, and mentor, but above all, friend. I admired her, and I loved her.

And I still want to be like her.

Allison Beasley

Bubbie Beasley

The thing I like to remember about Mrs. Ruth Kinnard is her love and respect for other people. She loved and respected every-one close to her – her husband, her children, her friends, her children's friends, her employees, etc. And so it was easy to love and respect her.

Mrs. Kinnard personified class, Southern style. The distinctive way she talked with that slow, sophisticated Alabama drawl, seemed to make the nice compliments she would pay other people sound even nicer. She would always ask about my parents – "Buubbie, how are Chaarlotte and Paidge"? Actually, my Dad's name, Padge, sounded odd. But the way she pronounced it with two or possibly three syllables, it seemed totally normal.

Mrs. Kinnard was always complimentary of other people. About my Dad she once said, "I really admire Padge Beasley because he always knows exactly how he feels about something." It later dawned on me that some people may have considered that just being opinionated.

An example of how Mrs. Ruth respected her elders was "Mr. Charlie," the older black gentleman who worked for her.

I liked the euphemism that Mrs. Kinnard used for the word "snake." She would not even say that word – she called them S's.

Once at toddy time we mixed a drink or two of Jim Beam. I admitted to Mrs. Kinnard that I had drunk entirely too much the night before. She told me not to feel guilty because it was ok to overindulge every so often. Trying to make me feel better she explained that her husband, Mr. Clay, once every year or so would go out to Steeple Morden, the guest house, and spend the night in solitude with a bottle of Jim Beam. She explained to me that this was a good way for a man to get in touch with his true thoughts. Well, I always remembered this; and much later in life when I was contemplating marriage, I used this method to make my decision. And thanks to Mrs. Kinnard's advice, I am now blessed with two beautiful children. I will always love and respect Mrs. Ruth Kinnard.

John P Beasley

Will Berry

RUTH MCDOWELL KINNARD........LIFE'S AMBITION

Ruth Kinnard was attracted to that in others which she
knew best about herself. She knew she was smart. There was no half
ground; if she brought you into her world, you joined in her ambition.
She was dogged in her pursuit. She had a vision not only for her life,
but also for what your life could be. She had high expectations of me
and of everyone else. She wanted life lived and lived fully. If she took
you seriously, then you had better get busy. We would have liked
each other no matter when we were first to meet, but as it was, I met
her when I was five at Mrs. Smith's kindergarten in Franklin where
Jon and I began a friendship that continues today. Mrs. Kinnard
wanted to know from the beginning where I was heading.

When I was eight, Wink and Judy and Paul Guffee started
Steeple Morden Day Camp, named for the little cottage at the back
of their house, "Martlesham Heath." "Steeple Morden," like the
Heath, was named for Mr. Clay's post in East Anglia during World
War II. Mrs. Kinnard believed houses and farms should have names,
and she liked, I think, the image certain words conjured when
strung together. It gave one a sense of her vision. And Martlesham
Heath was, as it sounds, a place more than a house. For in this
remodeled family home lying at the edge of Franklin off the
Lewisburg Pike across the pasture from "Carnton" and by the
Confederate Cemetery, extraordinary lives took place.

Mr. Clay's business, and how it revolutionized concrete pro-
duction and building in this country is central to this time, but to

talk of it is to take another's story. What I remember growing up among this family was the house. Decorated in the 1950's, it had a sense of style and taste that was not known in Franklin. It was international, sophisticated, of public rooms and spaces that flowed like the best Hollywood sets of the great and rich from the 1930's. It was tasteful, southern and gave me a sense of what style was. There was one other place that had that same focused elegance – "Farmington," the home of Ann and Donald Hart off Berry's Chapel Road going the other direction toward Nashville. Ann Hart and Ruth Kinnard were allies in life and remained close friends.

At the Heath I found my second home. I loved everything about it. That summer in 1962, after camp, I fell into life with the Kinnards. And until Jon and I graduated from BGA in 1972, I think I was there much of the time. It was during those long visits often lasting two days or more that Mrs. Kinnard and I would find time to talk. And here I came to know that I possessed an intelligence that she spoke to and insisted that I take seriously. Because she saw me, I followed her and became engaged with the idea of who I might be. I became ambitious.

Her house was a place where ideas were discussed and often served as a salon for her fellow students from Vanderbilt Law School. In 1969, we spoke of Kant and Kristofferson looking for insight into a world that was taking new shape. Her dinners were staged for thinking adults. At her table I found the joy of social recognition. Here I participated and learned the art of putting my thoughts into words. And although I was not always able, at that age, to support my first great declaration, I was encouraged to sit among them, an equal. My fondest memories of those years are of taking my place beside Mrs. Kinnard, listening.

My mother, too, had a particular vision and a similar uneasiness around people who did not think. She admired Ruth Kinnard enormously and would often remember out loud that she had known her at the University of Alabama when they were both freshmen. Ruth McDowell would be recognized: "She was handsome and had wavy blond hair. She wore thick glasses. I can see her across campus carrying a stack of books on her way to the library. Sometimes she just wouldn't see you. She was not a snob, she was near-sighted."

Mrs. Kinnard and my mother both understood the obligations of their lives in Franklin and brought to that tradition a sense of social responsibility. It is hard to imagine now after the collapse of family farming and the loss of so much open land, but in the late 1960's Franklin and Williamson County faced the first and, potentially, most devastating affront to their history. Before there was awareness in this country of the need to preserve our architectural legacy, many towns like Lebanon, Tennessee, abandoned their historic town centers to urban renewal. The past was eliminated. My mother recognized what was needed to safeguard the architectural gems of downtown Franklin. She understood that to protect the past it must be included in the future. With the gradual support of like – minded citizens, she helped create the Heritage Foundation of Franklin and Williamson County. Despite a growing enthusiasm, the early foundation was in trouble. There was vision but no workable structure. After a few dinner parties it was clear that if the Heritage Foundation did not take the lead in changing the perception of how Franklin should grow, nothing from the past could be saved.

I was part of those first gatherings, and I remember a morning when my mother went to see Mrs. Kinnard at her house to ask her to take the reins. My mother recalled later how Ruth was at first reluctant to take on the enormous responsibility of being president. She looked through the shoebox my mother had brought, names on index cards of a growing membership, a collage of that first year's efforts to establish the foundation, and with a sense of true bewilderment that I had come to understand as her inability to deal with other's lack of appreciation for detail, said "Oh Cripes, this is a mess. I'll do this for you, but I am going to have to redo everything." She did, and they set in motion an organization that can be credited with maintaining the beauty of downtown Franklin. My mother always gave Ruth Kinnard the credit for pulling the Heritage Foundation together and making it real.

On May 17th of 2001, the Heritage Foundation awarded Ruth McDowell Kinnard and Sue Douglas Berry a joint life – achievement award, acknowledging them as the founders of the Heritage Foundation of Franklin and Williamson County. As my mother dressed that afternoon for the ceremony, word came that Ruth Kinnard had died. My mother stopped what she was doing and heading back to bed said, "If Ruth's not going, I'm not going either." Sue Berry went to that awards ceremony alone. She died in November. My mother told me that there had never been anyone like Ruth Kinnard. She called her life a dynamic force. "A force," she said, "that will never be known again. No one will ever be able to do the things Ruth did."

Ruth McDowell Kinnard was my mentor. She taught me by her example that if I settled in life, then I had not really joined in; that I could re-invent myself as I moved toward that which I truly desired; that intelligence is strengthened through ambition.

Jeff Bethurum

Ruth Kinnard...one fine lady.

My first recollections of Ruth Kinnard date back to 1947 when I and several other Franklin kids began our first swimming lessons at Willow Plunge. Judy Kinnard, Wink Kinnard, Dickey Jewell, Padge Beasley and several other 3 and 4 year olds were studious members of that class. It is my recollection that it met every Tuesday and Thursday during the summer of 1947 (or maybe it was '48). Ruth was present or close by for most of these lessons and always made a special effort to make all of us feel at home. Bobby Gentry and Willie Howard Clark saw to it that the pool stayed in top shape.

Everyone is aware of Ruth's many accomplishments throughout her life. Her election to the Board of Mayor and Aldermen, however, is the accomplishment that brought us together as close friends. When I congratulated her on the night of her induction and addressed her as Mrs. Kinnard, she let me know emphatically that I should call her Ruth. I never made that mistake again. During her tenure, she was a leader in every way. Her wisdom and common sense added a depth to our board that we had not previously enjoyed. If she committed herself to a task, she always saw it to completion. If she agreed with me on an issue, I could always count on her vote. If she disagreed, I would often come over to her side. It was very rare for us to disagree. She treated everyone who came before the board with kindness and consideration, but she always had a backbone of steel. I once told her that I didn't think the Cool Springs Mall would amount to much. She replied, "Jeff, you might be wrong about that." I was.

When Cindy and I decided on Dec. 27th 1996 to get married on Dec. 28th 1996, the first call I made was to Ruth. Without hesitation she agreed to perform the ceremony. It was beautifully performed and characterized by sincerity that most preachers are incapable of. After A.J. was born, she became a friend of his as well. Here is a letter which she wrote him when he was 1 1/2 years old. It is classic Ruthie.

December 9, 2000
Dearest A.J.
Now that I can thread a needle again I have started back sewing. And I have made you a wedding handkerchief. Since I know that will be many years away and I may not be here then, I am asking your mother to keep it for your bride until then. In that way I can be a part of your wedding and I would like that.
With much love,
Ruthie

Our friendship remained close until her death and we all cherished it.

This world is a much better place because of Ruth's contributions, wisdom and love. Life has a way of confronting us with difficult decisions on a fairly regular basis. When making these decisions, I often find myself asking "What would Ruth do?"

Mitch Boult

Judge Kinnard was a member of our law firm for many years. She was always there to remind us to do the right thing, not just the profitable thing. She insisted that our lawyers do pro bono work, and initiated a pro bono program to ensure that indigent Nashvillians had family law representation. She walked the walk, too. She always carried a larger pro bono load than the rest of us. Thinking back on it, Judge Kinnard taught an entire generation of lawyers to give back.

Her special expertise was bankruptcy law. Personal bankruptcy is rock bottom in most lives; it involves the loss of everything, often including spouse and children. Judge Kinnard spent countless hours rehabilitating bankrupt clients, offering good legal advice and, more important, a shoulder to cry on, a sympathetic ear, suggestions for how to turn lives around. I think one reason her advice was so effective was that clients knew she had faced adversity courageously in her own life. In any event, some of our current titans of industry are Judge Kinnard's former clients, and they think she walked on water.

She always enjoyed a special relationship with the non-lawyers at our firm. One year she offered to "update" our employee manual. The rest of us didn't pay a lot of attention, and ever since, when somebody finds a provision that seems overly generous and exclaims "where the heck did that come from!?" – we say, "Judge Kinnard."

Judge Kinnard was the closest thing to a spiritual advisor that Jennifer and I had, so when we became engaged we asked her to officiate at our wedding. She agreed, and cheerfully made the 200 mile round trip to Livingston, Tennessee, for the ceremony. She spoke so movingly that even my callow groomsmen stopped leering at the bridesmaids, and teared up.

I think about Judge Kinnard often, wonder what she would have said or done at important moments, wish my children had known her.

Mitch Bault

Larimore Burton, Jr.

Ruth Kinnard was a woman of great courage! When I met her, she was a widow who as a mother still had a younger child at home. She was bright and smart yet she always listened to what everybody had to say – she was very perceptive, able to identify "truth" when she heard it.

I had been practicing law only for a few years when she asked me what Vanderbilt Law School was like. She shared her dream of moving her life forward with a law degree from Vanderbilt. I told her how wonderful I thought the law school education was, and I assured her she would love the challenge and that she would do well!

Her journey was a walk of excellence that took her through law school and in time as a skilled practicing attorney that included many productive years as a United States Bankruptcy Judge. It was indeed a privilege for me to know her and seek her counsel.

Larry Burton, Jr –

Karen Cagle

I worked with Ruth Kinnard for five short years and knew her for 12 years. I considered her to be a truly dear friend who never put herself first. She was always there for me with the perfect advice, whatever worries I may have had. She was one of the most caring, generous, wonderful people I have ever known. To this day, she looks down upon me from my mantle. No words can ever say what I feel for her – I miss her dearly.

Karen Cagle

Edie Caldwell

One summer's day in 1959, when I was 11 years old hanging out at Willow Plunge, my new friend Judy Kinnard invited me to go up to the house with her. I remember it, as if it were yesterday, for two distinct reasons. It was the first time I had been to a house that the entrance was through the laundry room (it was years before it dawned on me that there was a front door at the Heath) and the second was my meeting Miz Kinnard. I remember a blond blast of energy who seemed to be thrilled at the glorious opportunity to make my acquaintance. Heady stuff for an 11 year old. We became fast friends. Many years later, I named my first born child after her. Well sort of...we couldn't call him Ruthie, so we named him Claiborne in her honor.

She and I were very different. She was kind; I wasn't. She was generous and I wasn't. She admired my ability to say "no" to people, almost as much as I appreciated her capacity to always say "yes." Somewhere along the way, I realized that her way is better. I diligently try to be more like her now. It's not easy, but I'm working on it. Be kind, just be kind. It's my lesson learned over so many years with the indomitable Miz Kinnard. She is with me always and the world is a better place for having known her touch.

Edie Caldwell

Peggy Cardwell

RUTH, OUR FRIEND

I did not have the pleasure of knowing Ruth for the extended period that many knew her, but I cherish the years that I did know her and called her "Friend." When she became associated with Stokes & Bartholomew, we became friends. So often we would go to lunch and share our "family" stories. As mothers, we always had a child or grandchild story to share with each other.

One particularly funny story I remember is when Judy's daughter had colored her hair and the result was "dark burgundy." Judy was taking her to get some professional help at the salon. Ruth and I laughed about that and mentioned that we never knew what we would encounter when we raised children!

I know that we shared many of the same spiritual values, and we talked about those. Some days we "settled" the world's problems and I remember introducing her to one of my daughters, who was so impressed with her quick mind and how up-to-date she was on current events. She had many interests and she loved people. I doubt that she was ever really lonely because she had so many interests and so many friends with whom she shared her life. She always enjoyed a good book, and we shared those.

Professionally, we all know that she was the best. I will not try to expand on that. There are many others who can and, hopefully, will do that. Instead, I hope I can share some of the sweet and loving things that made her so special.

So many of us enjoyed the jams and jellies that she shared with us on special occasions. She knew just where to get the best fruit and looked forward to spending a weekend making these delicacies to share with her friends. How many of us have enjoyed using the crocheted dish cloths that she tucked into our Christmas present! The baby pillows that she made were to be cherished because of the loving stitches she put into them.

In a very special place in my home there is a beautiful handmade handkerchief that she made for my young grandson to give to his future bride on his wedding day. She made this even though he was a very small child at the time. She had so many ways of leaving her beautiful memories. All of her friends have shared in these gifts which were so much a part of her life and legacy. Yes, she left many greater and more complex gifts and memories, but behind all of the greatness was a lovely sweet southern lady who shared her love with many.

Peggy Cardwell

Cornelia Clark

I knew Ruth Kinnard as a role model, a mentor, a client and a friend. Knowing that she entered law school in the middle of her life, and at a time when women attorneys in Nashville were still a rarity, helped inspire me at age 26 to start my legal training. Seeing her succeed and excel as a judge made me know it was possible for other women to do the same thing. Her advice and counsel over the years were invaluable.

In her role as Franklin City Alderman she was a devoted public servant and a challenging client to advise and, when necessary, defend. Knowing that she would understand the law of a particular issue as well as I did inspired my preparation and made me a better lawyer on behalf of her and her colleagues. Her work to preserve and protect our history and heritage continues to benefit all the generations that follow.

Ruth's devotion to her professional work and her public avocations extended no less to her friendships. She was always available with a listening ear, a loving heart and a wicked wit. Her spirit is alive today in the public places that she helped preserve and in the hearts of all who called her friend. I am blessed to have been one of those people.

Connie Clark

Karin Coble

RUTH KINNARD – *much loved friend and inspiration…*

Having Ruth Kinnard as your friend was like having a surrogate mother, a therapist and a delightful buddy all in one – and the various roles never interfered with each other. How DID she do that?! From the time I first met Ruth in early 1977, she was my Friend. In fact, at lunch one day when we were discussing what in the world I might do to support myself, she, with her serious eyes, said "Why don't you go to law school?" (I suppose she thought that she did it, so why couldn't I.) And, not wanting to either disagree or disappoint her, I did! She was always an Inspiration.

Ruth was unusual in many respects, but one that especially impressed me was her ability to be always concerned with you and your well-being and/or problems without ever mentioning herself. She was amazingly "other person" oriented – surely part and parcel of her strong Christian beliefs. I know that life was not always easy or pleasant, but she neither sought pity, nor complained, nor burdened others with her trials and tribulations. And I never heard her speak disparagingly of another. I can't imagine anyone more perfectly suited to be a judge!

Ruth was always "up to" some good deed. When Gil Merritt was appointed to the 6th Circuit, Ruth, knowing how I enjoy cooking, hired me to plan and execute a party to celebrate the occasion. I remember very little about the event except that it was great fun, and she "rewarded" me with a beautiful amethyst necklace which I treasure. Her motive, of course, was to help me make a little money. I can't think of anything nicer than being remembered the way I remember Ruth: a smart, loving, compassionate, accomplished woman who was also great fun. I will always be grateful for her friendship and the time we spent together.

Karin Dale Coble

Lew Conner

My relationship with Ruth was that of friend and colleague at the Bar, a friend who made me feel as though she was my biggest fan.

I first came to know Ruth when she took the Tennessee Bar Review Course, part of which I taught in the late 1960s or early 1970s. She was one of the brightest and best of my students; and, of course, passed the bar with flying colors. Shortly thereafter, I received a copy of the nicest letter that I believe was ever written about me by anyone. Ruth had written the Dean of the Law School suggesting that I be hired as a full-time member of the faculty. Her thoughts about my perceived legal prowess and teaching skills, though mistaken, were much appreciated. Of course, she had by then already endeared herself to me.

From the moment I met her, I felt as though I had known her always. She was warm, gracious, caring and charming, and to me the epitome of a southern lady.

Over the years as a fellow member of the Bar I watched her grow and prosper with great pride. Of course, the highlight of her judicial career was her selection as a Federal Bankruptcy Judge, and she was one of the best. In her later years, I was fortunate for a short time to be in the same firm with her, of counsel to then Stokes & Bartholomew.

Ruth Kinnard was a very, very special person and a favorite of mine and so many others.

Lew Conner

Rev. Robert Cowperthwaite

I was Ruth's Priest for thirteen years.

Soon after we moved to Franklin from New York City, Ruth called me and said, "We need to get together and update your wills since you live in Tennessee now." She didn't even ask if we had another lawyer, if we already had wills — just knew that we needed her help. Generations of 12 year-olds were prepared for Confirmation by Ruth Kinnard. She provided a firm foundation for a faith that would often not be built on until much later in their lives. Her own faith was firm. On it she built a life of service to our Lord, to her family, her community and her profession. Hers was a life of dignity, respect, and faith. May we show our gratitude by living lives that respect the dignity of every human being.

Robert W Cowperthwaite

Linda Farrer

Legally Blonde

Over a span of thirty years, Ruthie played major roles in my life: mentor, judge, counselor, dear friend and confidant. Limited as we are by time and space to share the many warm, funny and wonderful memories of such an important and an overarching friendship, I must employ a metaphor to spark our collective and immediate memories of her warmth and color. While Ruthie loved literature the most, I know this metaphor of movies would elicit that wonderful warm deep hearty laugh that we all loved to hear. Four movies bring Ruthie to our hearts and minds because each portrays a stunningly beautiful, courageous and intelligent heroine with a stunning life philosophy: "Legally Blonde," "The Wizard of OZ," "Gone with the Wind," and "Emma."

Ruth M. Kinnard, a trust officer at Commerce Union Bank in Nashville, walked out of her office to greet me in 1970 with a white pique cotton suit, Ferragamo shoes and perfect handbag that would have made Elle Woods sweat. In the moments that followed, I was swept up in a current of spontaneity, laughter, wit and positive enthusiasm for life; the Law; Martlesham Heath; Franklin, Tennessee; Nashville and Vanderbilt University Law School. Immediately, we shared a love of the Episcopal Church, mystery novels and clearly "rack therapy." To appreciate the enormity of this successful sales campaign, the reader must know that I grew up in Sewanee, where in academics and basketball, Vanderbilt was a rival, and English Literature the path taken at SMU. Although I knew women could be doctors, my trips to the Franklin County Courthouse never provided me with a glimpse of a glamorous lawyer like Ruth

M. Kinnard. Like Elle Woods, Ruth's force and presence made practicing law not only look like fun, and well-dressed, but essential. So, entirely because of my interest in the "essential" and the good work that my mentor told me that I could do, I woke up one morning and decided to go to law school.

Everyone remembers the person who gave them their first real job. Mine was to be sworn in by The Hon. Ruth M. Kinnard, Judge, as a receiver in bankruptcy. Judge Kinnard recruited new lawyers to the U.S. Bankruptcy Court as trustees and receivers under the then "new rules," a watershed event. Called into her chambers, Judge Kinnard sat at her desk piled high with files, a cigarette and her monogrammed RMK silver cigarette case in her left hand, a fountain pen in her right hand, writing on a yellow pad in her familiar large script, trying to light her cigarette and answering the phone all at once. She welcomed me with a huge smile and a chuckle and, as I raised my right hand, swore me in as a receiver in bankruptcy. In a voice reminiscent of my grandmother offering me homemade ice cream, Judge Kinnard instructed me to go out and seize a business, lock it up, post formal Bankruptcy signs on the building, inventory the multi-ton machines and make my return within the time stated on the Order. She informally offered that she did not think I needed a gun, but better take a hammer. Like Dorothy in "The Wizard of Oz," she helped us find heart, courage and means and humor to face our life and career challenges.

As young lawyers, she trained us well and invited us to parties and dinners at her beloved home, Martlesham Heath. She encouraged us to work hard and contribute to the Law, the Church and Nashville. She supported enthusiastically Jim Farrer's work in psychiatry and early on took an active interest in the developments in that area of medicine. Her court hearings were human drama: the life predicament. Her graciousness and compassion suffused a courtroom and soothed a farmer who wept when recounting that the medical bills from his wife's illness and fight with cancer brought him to her courtroom. Alert to mischief and always a teacher, she judiciously instructed trustees to sell and bank officers to file liens. She was not Scarlett O'Hara, although just as spirited and lively, but Melanie Hamilton, full of prayerful compassion for human suffering and kindness to everyone who came to know her and to her courtroom. Whether in court or in friendship, she offered her intellect, compassion, friendship, advice and help openly and generously. Active with civic work for which she won many awards, she was never too tired or to busy to lend advice on a legal issue or life issue. Judge Kinnard, like Melanie, believed in the goodness of people. Her Christianity informed her work and life and gave her joy. And like Scarlett's Melanie, she had only good things to say about people – hedged a little bit maybe – but positive and good.

In human relations, there is always someone who surveys the landscape and, like a gardener, knows where plants will thrive. Often, it is a pairing of plants or an unusual combination of flowers that take the garden from early spring into late autumn and achieves a splendor that only happens every few years. Ruthie could see that landscape and, like Emma, loved being matchmaker whether for business, friends, or husband and wife. The fixin' up might be as subtle as a luncheon for two friends who did not know each other, but both with children of the same age; or, focusing on the talents of someone whose parents thought they had none, enthusiastically convinced them the talents were there. The list is endless and all of us know who we are. For me the fixin' up took place on the day Nixon resigned. While I was visiting friends in Ardmore, Pa., Ruthie suggested that I call her daughter, Judy, who was working at the Philadelphia Inquirer. She thought we would enjoy each other. The problem was that I didn't know which daughter I was meeting: Tia or Judy. We did not meet until two years later. As for the two daughters, I finally got the facts straight by asking which daughter was the elder, Tia or Judy. Ruthie laughed long and hard, because there were not two daughters! Ruthie made sure that I met Judy and Chris because somehow, in her own wisdom, she knew not only that our families would become great friends, but that we would need each others' support and love over the years: life's predicament again. Chris and Judy became Matthew Farrer's Godparents, and I became Elizabeth's godmother. Andrew and Matthew Farrer referred to Ruthie as Dar Dar (Heath's and Elizabeth's name for Ruthie) and remembered her every Christmas when they would hang the personalized wooden ornaments that she sent on the Christmas tree. And as our families' friendship grew, I began to call Judge Kinnard, Ruthie.

Living away from Tennessee, I began to see Ruthie through the eyes of my children, her daughter and son-in-law and grandchildren. We would talk on the phone from time to time and always close with: I love the Law and I love the Lord and, then she would say "I love you, darlin'." Like Elle Woods, Ruthie's infectious, positive attitude helped me achieve career goals while her match making skills paved the way for life-long friendships. And, in spite of everything she went through, similar to Melanie, she saw compassion and love, forgiveness, ground for growth and renewal, and great potential and goodness. For Ruthie there was no place like home – her Franklin, Tennessee, but above all she loved the Lord.

Linda V. Farrer

Doug Fisher

Memories of Ruth, a friend since the 40's:

Late 40's: Ruth is married to my boss, Claiborne Kinnard, who is recently back from the war and is managing Willow Plunge in Franklin, where he has hired me to lifeguard. Ruth brings Judy and Wink to the pool weekday mornings when the crowds are thin. She spreads out her towels on the grassy bank that slopes down to the pool and gossips with other young Franklin mothers while some of their children take swimming lessons. Her husband is peeved with her. She has had an artist paint his portrait from a photograph. "Can you imagine her spending money on something that silly while I am putting every nickel I've got into the block plant?"

Early 50's: Ruth is national president of the Tri Delt's and often has young female guests to Franklin from out of state. She sees that each one is taken to dinner, sometimes by me. Occasionally I remind her that my Willow Plunge salary was $25 a week.

Middle 60's: After her husband's death, Ruth enrolls in the law school at Vanderbilt. About two years after her 1970 graduation U.S. District Judge Frank Gray, Jr. of Franklin appoints her to the federal bankruptcy bench, where she gets a reputation as a quick study.

One day I am in bankruptcy court. Ruth is on the bench. A bankruptcy lawyer standing before her has filed a mindless pleading. She is holding it. Her hands are trembling and her face is red as she tells him what can befall him.

1978: Julie and I move from Nashville to downtown Franklin. We affiliate with St. Paul's where Ruth instructs a confirmation class. Our daughter Rachel attends the class. Rachel is walking home after

Holly Hines

Holly Hines

her first communion. She says to Julie:

"Do you know what I was thinking when I took communion?"

"What were you thinking?"

"There goes my liver."

90's and later: Ruth is living in her Franklin apartment one block down the street from our house (and the almost-next-door home of our neighbors Jon, Laura and Campbell Kinnard). Ruth and I participate in some of the same lawyer groups that have evening functions in Nashville. Ruth, Julie and I drive to Nashville together to attend. On the way Ruth always brings up some mutual acquaintance and observes "Isn't [he/she] *simply wonderful?*"

Doug Fisher

Tish Fort

If I were looking for a friend I would look for Ruth Kinnard. She had the rare quality of always being secondary in our times together; and for a lady who dedicated part of her professional life to being a federal judge, Ruth, never, never made me feel she was judging my actions or my sentiments.

Alas, if only...if only I could have had two mothers, if only I could have had four sisters.

Sarah Alexander Green

For the last 20 years or so, thinking women have had Justice O'Connor as a role model. I have had Ruth Kinnard as my role model for about 45 years. I strongly believe I have had the better/best ROLE MODEL! All of my growing-up years in Franklin, Tennessee (which I still call home), I saw Mrs. Kinnard as the pillar of St. Paul's Episcopal Church. Hers is the face I see when I go back to my Sunday School days or recall St. Paul's Church. I will always remember Ruth asking when I was going to have my sons, Michael and David, baptized. It was important to Ruth that I attend to that and because she urged me to – Michael and David were baptized at St. Paul's Episcopal Church. Mama and Daddy had a special luncheon for the boys' honor. The Godparents, family and friends came to Isola Bella, and Ruth was the guest of honor. What a blessing to us all is Ruth Kinnard!

Oh, my goodness, what a flood of memories come back when I think of Mrs. Kinnard: Willow Plunge, the Middle Tennessee Pony Club (I can still diagram the parts of a horse or rather label them), sitting behind Judy and Wink in Church (thinking Judy the most beautiful girl with the most beautiful hair), Mrs. Kinnard taught Sunday School and I believe she taught me the Apostle's Creed. More stream of consciousness memories: Su-Su broke her leg riding out at Martlesham Heath; Samson and Delilah; coldest pool and worst sunburn; best fudge pie! God Bless you, Mrs. Kinnard!

I think growing up in Franklin, Tennessee in the 50's and 60's was a unique and awesome experience.

Sarah

Marian Harrison

Ruth Kinnard was my mentor, my friend, and my "mother."

I first met Ruth – then Judge Kinnard to me – when I clerked for Chief Judge Frank Gray, Jr., in Nashville. Almost every day of my two years there, we clerks (I, Bill Aiken, and then Dewees Berry) lunched with Judge Kinnard and Judge Gray and often had dinner with them also. Just as Judge Gray was clearly smitten with Ruth and pressed her later to marry him, I too was in awe of this bright judge who had tackled law school later in life and then almost immediately had jumped into the job of bankruptcy judge. I was then only beginning to understand how strong and fine this gracious lady was.

Ruth declined Judge Gray's entreaties to marry, choosing instead to continue as bankruptcy judge and to concentrate on her family and friends. After I entered the practice of law, I was still a regular on Ruth's lunch card, taking my questions and problems to her as a mentor. After Judge Gray fell ill and then died, Ruth's judgeship was not renewed with the changing of the guard at the federal courthouse. She dealt with her displacement as usual with grace in public even though she was hurt and angry. In contrast, I loudly expressed my anger. When Ruth began to practice law, she insisted that I call her Ruth, although even at the end, I frequently slipped in a "Judge Kinnard" or two.

After Ruth began practicing law, she was still a mentor, but gradually we began to share the ups and downs of law practice. You could say she was becoming more of an equal – more my friend than mentor. Our lunches and our frequent telephone calls and dinners led to friendship for sure, but also to a third role in my life – my "mother." I remember an early lunch one day in her office when she brought out 12 almonds, cottage cheese, and water for us. As I grabbed more than half the almonds, thinking they were hor d'oeuvres, she said sternly – "only six." "We," she said, "are this day beginning the Scarsdale Diet, and it calls for only six almonds at this meal." While I do not remember now if Scarsdale was the diet "we" were embarking upon, I do remember how adamant she was that "we" were going to lose weight. Now, truthfully, she did not need to lose weight but had clearly set out to provide an example for me – just like a good mother. I confess that I have not been as good at following through on Ruth's diet lesson as I have some of her other lessons over the years.

Ruth's motherly lessons expanded as did her legal lessons and our friendship. I learned to pour coffee for guests in her living room after dinner, as well as her scotch before dinner. My dressing for the practice of law improved with her guidance, as did my manners. I cannot say that I ever absorbed her grace – her grace was clearly an unobtainable mark – her graciousness was a great influence nevertheless. She, to me, was the epitome of the good mother – gracious but strong, compassionate but firm.

All Ruth's roles in my life came to bear upon my quest for a federal judgeship. Through my several failed efforts over the years, she coached and pushed me as a mentor, supported me as her friend, and consoled me as a mother. When in 1999, I was appointed a bankruptcy judge, she seemed more excited than my colleagues, my friends, and even my real parents.

When four years ago Ruth was on her deathbed and in a coma, I went to see her and sat by her side holding her hand while Judy, John, and Wink, left briefly to run errands. I remember I was dressed in khakis and a casual shirt, which I had worn to the courthouse that day. It may have been my imagination, knowing how she would view my unjudgely dress that made me think that she "rolled her eyelids," and I apologized for it. I could just hear her saying "now Marian – are all the women lawyers wearing pants like that now?" Ruth was always kind and graciously prodding, seeking to help me be a better lawyer, judge, and yes, lady. I will be forever grateful to Ruth as mentor, Ruth as friend, and Ruth as mother.

Marian F. Harrison

Ann Wright Hart

The Lord blessed me with many friends but of all of them Ruth Kinnard stands out! Her caring and concern for others made her a very special human being. Her wisdom and her willingness to share it with those less fortunate. Not only was she brilliant but she used that brilliance to others' advancement. I was devoted to her, and I miss her very much.

I first met Ruth when she came to Franklin as a bride. It was at the Nashville home of Clay's aunt, Mrs. Bolling Warner (Anne Kinnard), where we first met. She was a friend of my mother, Mrs. Malvern Wright, and she invited me to lunch to meet her new niece, Ruth McDowell Kinnard. She was young as was I at the time, and we became friends and our friendship continued through the years. Not only did she teach Sunday school at the Episcopal church in earlier years, but she made the decision to go to Law School and was later appointed to the Federal Bench. This alone shows how her wisdom was respected.

A devoted wife to Claiborne Kinnard until his death, she ran their farm Martlesham Heath with the help of devoted servant Mary Taylor in the kitchen and "Mister Charlie" on the grounds and at their swimming pool.

It was after Clay's death that she entered Vanderbilt Law School and went on to become the first female Federal judge in the state of Tennessee.

Ann W. Hart

Elaine Husband

An inspired admirer, daughter of a life-long friend, Helen Hudgins

I did not see Ruth a great deal after I "grew up." As a child, I believe I was in love with her, her gracious spirit, and her flair for life. Her friendship with our family was marked by generosity and love. Many times she played the important role of encourager and mentor to us as children and young adults. She meant the world to my mother, Helen Hudgins, and their friendship was strong to the very end. In their last years of life, they were fortunate to be neighbors within walking distance as their worlds grew smaller. No, Ruth Kinnard and my mother never had small worlds, just limited mobility to get around in them.

My sister, Robin, was a special favorite of Ruth's. (Everybody who knew Ruth thought they were a special favorite, I'm sure.) If my facts are straight, when Robin left for Auburn University, Ruth founded a Tri Delta Sorority chapter just so she would have the opportunity to be a part of something Ruth felt would enrich her college years. I have found letters of recommendation from her, sealing Robin's chances for membership. The woman could accomplish anything!

My most vivid memory of Ruth, and the positive impact she had on me as a child, occurred the night of my sister Robin's rehearsal dinner at Martlesham Heath, the Kinnard's lovely home. Surrounded by beauty and laughter, I was feeling very grown up for a nine year old little sister. Allowed to wear tiny high-heeled shoes, I waltzed around the sumptuous dining table while being served delicious food. As I turned to walk to my chair, I tripped, fell and agonized as I watched my tray, Ruth's china, and my life pass before me. I wanted to disappear into the oriental rug, but only managed to make it to the bathroom where I hid and cried. Ruth appeared with an understanding smile and arms opened wide to console me and assure me that "that 'ol rug didn't mean a thing to her compared to me." She wiped my eyes and led me by the hand out of the powder room into a room full of people who must have received orders from her not to even look my way. The magic night was not spoiled by my flying salmon croquette after all.

Elaine H. Gerhard

Dick Jewell

It was the mid 1970's and I had moved back from Knoxville and was living in Nashville. I started attending St. Bartholomew's Episcopal Church on Belmont Park Terrace where Chuck Murphy was the Senior Rector. He and his wife, Ann, had changed the normal flow of events by introducing an early Monday thru Friday morning service and breakfast called "6:15." One morning I was late and walked in to see Ruth Kinnard sitting at the breakfast "square" table enjoying a cup of coffee. I can't remember if her "Judgeship" had ended or she was in private practice. I wasn't at all surprised to see her but she may have been surprised to see me. It was in my early teen days that she and Clay Kinnard invited our church youth group to their house for fellowship time. We reconnected and the conversation turned to St. Paul's Episcopal Church in Franklin. The subject of Senior Rector, Father Ray, came up. She agreed with me that Father Ray, "Daddy Rabbit," as he was often known, predated the titled Juvenile Director of Franklin, because he allowed a "pool table" in the basement of the church and barricaded the side street for combo parties. I was able to enjoy her company for many mornings as we shared our faith and many answers to prayer. Then one morning, Wink showed up with her. This went on for quite some mornings. What I remember most was Ruth Kinnard's willingness and openness to share about herself and her deep faith.

Willow Plunge:

After my father died in 1979, Mother decided to be nearer to her beloved golf club at Carnton Plantation so she bought a lot on

Kinnard Drive and built one of the first houses. One day while checking on the construction, I walked across the road and ventured down to the old abandoned Willow Plunge site which still held the remains of that wonderful fun-in-the-sun place for me. The dressing rooms and pavilions were gone but the sloping hill and demolished pool shells were still distinguishable. The catwalk between the pools had a gaping hole in it. As I made my way through the overgrown weeds and dense thicket, I couldn't help but think about all the good times that I had swimming and playing on these very grounds. This was the place where I learned to swim from Sissy Roberts and watched Robert Inman, Tandy Rice and Mike Hudgins lifeguard from their tall perched seats in the sky or so it seemed. Many times they would "show-off" their diving skills by jumping from the high diving board to the lower one, a feat that was never allowed by the young swimmers.

As I walked across the catwalk, I remembered the days when the little pool was at low-water, and the girls would lie out on blankets on the white concrete because the sun was hotter and the tanning was better, I guess. It was sad to see the remaining concrete slabs where the dressing rooms once stood. I made my way up the walkway to see what I could find, and there it was, the old "putt-putt" golf course still visible, even across the ditch for the more difficult holes. As I made my way up the hill, I noticed the foundation remains where the old game room was. The "bear shoot," as I called it, was a game where one would use a guided-beam rifle to shoot a moving bear. In the bear's midsection was a glass circle and the object was to hit the bear so he would rise up, growl, and change direction, quickly. This attraction held an extra risk. If you were wet from just swimming and had not dried off, the moisture would create a ground and the electrical connection would give you a little shock. It was cool to endure it anyway. The next attraction that I remember was a stamp-type machine that you could emboss letters on an aluminum star-like disc. One would spell out the desired message by pulling the lever down and embossing the disc. It was cool to hang that disc on a chain around your neck. Moving on and much to my surprise the lattice-shaped concession hut was still visible with some imagination. I could just taste the chess pies, hamburgers, tomato sandwiches… cold drinks…Orange Crush was my favorite. They had it all, but "no swimming" after you ate was the rule.

These were my earliest happiest days because just getting to Willow Plunge was exciting. The ride out Lewisburg Pike meant that you got to jump the railroad tracks just past the diary dip (Gilco) and then you were looking for the white railed fence on the right. The gate box where you paid to enter was next and then a short drive down the gravel road to park on the grass beside the screened-in pavilions. We had many birthday parties in those pavilions and as I got into high school, combo parties (bands) often played there… plenty of room to park and plenty of room to dance.

On one occasion, a birthday party, Clay Kinnard drove a tractor pulling a big trailer. We all jumped on and he drove us up the field to the Confederate Cemetery and back. I have a Polaroid picture of just such a ride.

As I left the grounds and headed back toward Kinnard Drive, I couldn't help but hear the loudspeaker calling somebody to the phone or music being played…Doris Day, Les Paul and Mary Ford or the laughter of boys rolling inner tubes down the hill to the pool… and even a smile, remembering the times a few guys climbed over the fence and had a cool midnight swim. Those days are gone for now but maybe they can be relived again…with a Willow Plunge Reunion!

Thanks to the Kinnard family, the Gentry brothers, the concession ladies who cooked those great meals, and all the lifeguards, swim instructors and employees who gave us all a little piece of Heaven around a "cement pond" in Franklin, Tennessee.

Dick Jewell

Bill King

"Bill King!" Did I ever once see Ruth Kinnard without hearing my own name with the largest of exclamation marks following it? Did anybody?

Ruth's signature greeting – your own name writ large – made you feel special before you sat down with her and felt even more special. When she said my wife Robin's name, it was one long and wonderful, "Robbinnn!" I loved hearing her say it. Ruth had us all before hello. Forget the hollow pleasantries – It was your name, followed by the best of hugs, followed by the conversations most of us treasure today as much as we did the day they took place.

Of course it was sometimes a challenge to get a two-way conversation going with Ruth. William Shawn, the legendary Editor of *The New Yorker*, was honored after his death in 1992 with a number of remembrances not unlike those in this book. Several of the magazine's writers mentioned the fact that no one could ever remember getting out of an elevator behind "Mr. Shawn." His unfailing politeness made him constitutionally unable to walk out of an elevator before his colleague did.

It must have been frustrating to *New Yorker* staffers who spent entire careers failing to confer upon William Shawn such a minor courtesy.

I know how they felt. That's how I always felt when, during the quarterly lunches we shared for years and years and years, I tried to get Ruth to tell me what was going on *her* life before she had fully wheedled out of me every iota of what was going on in mine. *This*

time, I'd say to myself, I'm going to find out how Judy and Wink and Jon are doing, right up front. "How's Marian?!," Ruth would open with, asking about my Mom. I never got the bead on her. Surely it would have been easier to follow William Shawn out of an elevator than it was to follow Ruth's story with your own.

And what an extraordinary listener she was! My sons never had the privilege of knowing Ruth, but she knew everything about them: How was Will liking NYU? Was he using the French he'd picked up while an exchange student? Was Josh still dating Ashley, or had Boulder brought a new girlfriend into his life? Ruth was interested like no one I've ever encountered in the smallest details of what made you who you are. She didn't need to know your children to be interested in them; it was enough that she knew you.

When I first met Ruth Kinnard she was really old. At least that's what those of us in the Vanderbilt Law School Class of 1970 thought when we met her those first weeks of September, 1967. Ruth was 48. She was one of three women in a class of nearly a hundred. It's hard to imagine being so outnumbered today, when law school classes are pretty much balanced by gender, and when racial diversity is so much greater than it was then. Nor were the three women in our class your typical Vanderbilt coeds. Besides Ruth, a woman over twice our age, there was Rita, an African-American woman who became one of Ruth's closest law school friends, and there was Susan, a sightless woman, undaunted by the additional challenges unknown to the look-alike guys of Vandy Law.

I realize now why that class was especially close. It wasn't because of the raging Vietnam War, which law school was allowing many of us to studiously avoid, and it wasn't some sort of camaraderie that flows naturally from being tossed together in an alien and challenging environment. It was Ruth. Far from being a middle-aged misfit in a sea of high-performing recent college grads, she was the soul of our class. She invited us to the Heath for our parties. She was the first friend we wanted our parents to meet when they came to town. She listened to our twenty-something nonsense, and, while always playing down her own abilities (laughing at times about even

69

the appropriateness of her being there), somehow managed to out-perform most of us in class and in grade point.

What a classy woman! What an incredible influence in our lives! What a pole star to follow!

Years ago, late in the seventies, someone wrote a Newsweek piece titled, "Second Acts in American Lives." It celebrated a then-new phenomenon: people changing careers late in life, and finding fulfillment in doing so. I sent it to Ruth, who was just beginning that second act after a successful run as wife and mother. I didn't know at the time that she'd only just begun. There were other acts: lawyer, banker, mediator, loft apartment-living urbanite, judge, pulp mystery expert, and probably nine or ten other acts that she never told me about. There was her spiritual life, deep and serious, yet known to many of us only on the surface – the cross around her neck, the daily stops at St. Bart's on the way to work, the decades of faithfulness to those lucky St. Paul's confirmation classes.

Anybody who wasn't inspired by Ruth Kinnard quite obviously never knew her. To know her was to be grateful, just for that.

Bill Koch

Ruth Kinnard: Friend and Inspiration.

Law school, like life, doesn't come with operating instructions. You show up on the first day with little idea what lies ahead but with the hope that you can avoid falling on your face until you get your bearings. While you're prepared to rely on your ingenuity and wits – after all you're going to be a lawyer – you're secretly hoping that someone who has already been through it will take the time to show you where the opportunities and obstacles are.

As it turned out, I did not have to find a guide through my first year of law school. Vanderbilt provided me one, Ruth Kinnard. And what a guide she was, not just through that first year of law school, but through most of my professional and personal life. Over the years, her kindness, gentleness, and candor kept me on course. Her encouragement and support enabled me to go farther than I thought possible.

Ruth was not the third-year advisor I was expecting. Far from being tall and assertive, Ruth was diminutive and genteel. She was a true Southern lady, the sort of lady whose acquaintance I had made while reading William Faulkner's novels during my senior year of college. My two most vivid memories of Ruth following our first meeting were that she smiled with her eyes and that something in her manner left me with the belief that I really mattered to her, even though there was no reason why I should have. She was "old South;" I was "not from here." She was connected; I was untethered. She had nothing to gain by investing her energy or interest in me, but she did nonetheless.

My time at Vanderbilt was beginning just as Ruth's was ending, and our paths diverged after she graduated and moved on to begin her legal career. We did not see each other again until two or three years following my graduation from law school. A mutual friend of ours, not knowing our relationship during law school, invited both of us to dinner, thinking that we would like each other. That dinner marked the beginning of a thirty-year friendship that continues to this day.

Over the years, there have been countless excursions to the movies, dinners with friends, sharing holiday celebrations, and supporting each other in times of sorrow. Ruth helped mark the milestones of my life. Her presence provided a valediction for the proceedings – whatever they were.

While Ruth had some definite ideas about how things should be, she never presumed to impose her views on others. It would never have occurred to her to be didactic or preachy. She taught by example without intending to; although she was not above giving a gentle nudge every once in a while. The two most enduring lessons I learned from Ruth were the delight and wisdom to be derived from remaining curious and the peacefulness to be derived from faith.

For many, living a long life narrows horizons and diminishes opportunities. The years fold in on themselves, and the known and relevant world shrinks. Ruth's horizons remained broad to the last. There was always something to be learned or explored. Just about anything (within reason) was worth trying at least once. Debby and I were lucky to be in on many of these explorations, and our spirits were buoyed by Ruth's child-like delight at experiencing something new, no matter what it was. One night when we dropped her off following one of these excursions, Ruth observed that "this has been the best day ever." Our hearts leapt at these words, and they leap today remembering them.

Ruth's faith gave her an aura of peacefulness. She did not need to proclaim it; you could feel it in her presence. Hers was not the "pie in the sky by-and-by" sort of faith. It was a faith, tested by tragedy, that instilled a firm belief that God would never heap burdens upon us that we would not be able to carry with His help. Ruth carried her burdens, and the burdens of others, with grace and hope and faith that in the fullness of time, all things would come out where they should. While all of us are created in God's image, I saw His image more clearly in Ruth than in anyone else.

I was a stranger in a strange land, and Ruth took me in. She allowed me to share part of her rich and nuanced life. She took Debby to her heart, and she cared for us without reservation or condition. Each of us yearns to be truly known and to be accepted by those whom we love. The greatest gift is knowing that we have been truly known and accepted. Ruth knew Debby and me, and her greatest gift to us was her love and acceptance.

Words spoken in love are remembered, and acts done with kindness remain. Ruth's words and acts will always remain a part of me. Even though she has joined the company of the saints in light, I live my life firmly believing that I am a better person for knowing Ruth and that one day, we will pick up where we left off. What a joyful meeting that will be.

Debby Koch
Friend and Admirer

BRILLIANT, BELOVED RUTH

This is hard. I think of myself as a writer, at least that's more or less how I make my living. But writing about Ruth Kinnard and what she means to me is almost too hard because it needs to be perfect. Not because she would ever expect it to be that way, but because I want anyone who reads these words to somehow understand what an extraordinary lady she was, to gain a glimpse of what a true friend looks like, and to feel the profound power of her life.

When the unimaginable happened and Ruth died, she left a devoted family, a legion of friends, and countless colleagues and admirers who continue to mourn her loss, rejoice in the fact that they were a part of her life, and miss her deeply. I was so very proud that I was her friend.

Holidays will never be the same without Ruth for Bill and me. For nearly twenty five-years we celebrated every important occasion together – each of our birthdays and anniversaries…and, every year she came for *Christmas Eve Soup* bearing pretty bags full of home-made jelly. She must have cooked up a million jars of jelly. And, no matter what the weather, or the personal stresses that this season can bring, we always had such a wonderful time. We laughed and laughed and had spirited discussions about every conceivable subject. Best of all, being with Ruth at Christmas was the finest reminder one could have of what the celebration is really all about. There were hard times too. I thought my own heart would break for Ruth when Clay died. Looking up and seeing her at my parents' funerals made me feel as if an angel had come to help give them just the right send-off. She helped me to believe in Heaven.

She and I exchanged murder mysteries and we liked to go to movies that made us smile...not the profound ones that made you contemplate weighty and important matters or the violent ones where you thought a pet or a person might really have gotten hurt. When she found out that I was having trouble sleeping, she gave me a little neck pillow with a handmade lace cover. It's a bit worn and tattered now and still I hug it close every night and say a sweet good-night to Ruthie.

She was brilliant. And even though they weren't, Ruth always thought others were smarter than she and wanted to learn from them. When we saw each other she'd ask how I was and listen intently to my answer because she was interested in it. But with those preliminaries out of the way, she'd then say in that gravelly voice which I still hear in my head, *"Now Debby, what does Judge Koch think about..."* and it would be the hot topic of the day which she probably already knew more about than (Ellen Pollack excepted) all the rest of my friends put together. She loved Bill and was so proud of him and thought he was just the smartest man she knew. She always wanted to know what his point of view was, as if to supplement and reinforce the validity of her own.

Someone from the Nashville Bar asked me to write a Memorial Resolution with which they could honor her life at their Annual Meeting. I wrote page after page after page of biographical information about her beloved family, her days at *Martlesham Heath*, her civic involvement, and her many, many professional achievements and accomplishments.

I ended it with the following – my own personal thoughts and observations – which I hope give a sense of her style, her elegance, her goodness, her being:

One of Ruth's lesser-known endeavors was her effort to introduce New York style living to Franklin. During her later years she took up residence as an urban pioneer in an exquisitely decorated, second floor townhouse on Main Street in Franklin, directly above several shops. She loved living downtown and could often be seen walking to this store or that restaurant and greeting virtually everyone she passed by name. She always had time for people and never failed to stop and ask about their families or their work or something else that was important to them.

Ruth was a lovely and gracious lady who never lost her childlike curiosity nor her enchantment with learning. She was a faithful correspondent whose notes and letters were treasured by their recipients. She was a gifted writer and an avid reader who could be found variously pouring over a scholarly legal tome or burning the midnight oil on a hot new murder mystery.

She was gentle and genteel with an independent nature and an iron will. She was an excellent lawyer whose clients got every ounce of her attention and the best legal advice available because she was always focused on serving their needs first, and making a living second or third. She was a treasured mentor to many of Tennessee's best and brightest attorneys and a fierce advocate for their profession. She loved the law.

Ruth was the best friend a person could have. She was unfailingly interested, unconditionally loyal, and always, always there for you when you needed her. When you were with her she gave you the gift of peace, no matter what was swirling around in your life. She was infinitely kind.

She loved to garden and go to movies and was passionate about music – from Franz Liszt to Lyle Lovett. She made plum jelly and tatted lace and dispensed justice, all with an even hand.

Ruth was profoundly religious and rarely seen without her exquisite golden cross nestled close to her heart. She attended Mass every day and carried her deeply held beliefs with her in whatever she undertook. She loved angels and, to those who knew her, she was one.

Ruth Kinnard was a Renaissance Woman:

– a southern belle who married a war hero;

– a loving Mother, Grandmother and Godmother of three children, six grandchildren and at least sixteen godchildren;

– a pioneer among women in the legal profession and the Federal judiciary;

— a dedicated civic and government leader in Franklin and Nashville, and,

— a beautiful and generous and loving and sensitive person whose extraordinary impact on her family and friends and peers and partners will never be matched nor forgotten.

While those of us who labor on would have had her linger with us a while longer, Ruth's work on Earth is done. She has borne the gladness of the Gospel to young and old. She has claimed the high calling. She has kept the faith. She rests now, having been welcomed with His words: Well done, good and faithful servant. To which we say Amen and Amen!

I love you Ruth. You touched my soul. I will never stop missing you.

Ashby Patterson Koch

Calvin Lehew

There is a law in metaphysics that says we are drawn to people like ourselves. It is called the Law of Attraction. From the first time I was introduced to Ruth Kinnard I knew that despite our age difference we had much in common.

She truly treated all alike no matter if they were wealthy or poor, black or white, had status and position in the community or not. She respected all living beings. She thought "outside the box" and it was always positive and for the good of all. I felt comfortable being in her presence even though I looked up to her in so many ways.

I loved to listen to her talk about her husband, Clay Kinnard. She referred to him as a "brave, daring, adventurous soul" and she kept his picture above their fireplace with him dressed in his flight gear. Because I am a pilot she loved telling me how he flew missions in World War II and was engaged in aerial combat. I would hang on to every word.

She had a strong influence in my preservation efforts. Years ago I had just been chosen to be the youngest person appointed on the board of directors of the oldest and largest bank in Williamson County. My first accomplishment was in talking the board into not tearing down a row of beautiful "old" buildings north of the square on Third Avenue for a parking lot. Ruth was happy that I did that.

Later I was asked who I would recommend for a new board member as we had a vacancy. I made the pitch that we should be the first to put a woman on the board of directors. The committee did not like my idea but asked who I would pick. I immediately thought and said Ruth Kinnard. It would be many years later before a woman was placed on the board.

She was a wonderful friend and I miss her positive, creative energy.

Marty Ligon

Many pleasant thoughts come to my mind in Williamson County and Franklin about Mrs. Claiborne Kinnard, affectionately known to most as Ruth or Ms. Ruth.

My most memorable times with Ms. Ruth were in St. Paul's Episcopal Church. She loved St. Paul's and dedicated a good portion of her life to the young people of St. Paul's and particularly her leadership in the "Confirmation Class." She was a very striking lady. She always wore a dress to church and was known for the large, gold cross that hung on a heavy, gold chain around her neck. My closest association with Ruth was between 1974 and 1985, when I served as her assistant teacher of her sixth grade Confirmation Class.

I asked the children of Martin and Judy Simmons to share some of their thoughts about Ms. Ruth, since all three children were in her class and were touched by her.

Carter said: "What so clearly impacted me as a young candidate for confirmation is that Ms. Kinnard taught us the meaning of faith, not by just telling us to have it but by showing us she had it. Of course, she was eloquent and persistent in the way she spoke about such things as 'Acts of Faith' – like how to make the Sign of the Cross and how to genuflect. However, I was mostly taken by the unwavering faith she showed in her eyes, her smile, her big voice and her connection to the cross she wore around her neck every Sunday."

Alison Simmons Wingo said: "I have so many wonderful memories of Mrs. Kinnard – mostly from my sixth grade confirmation class and learning the different colors and seasons of the church – and

83

after its completion, receiving my first Book of Common Prayer with such pride. I will always remember her being a constant figure in the second pew on the right-hand side of the church every Sunday and wearing that big, bright cross necklace that seemed so heavy, especially in her last years. But by far, my favorite memory of Mrs. Kinnard is when she leaned over my first son, born over eight years ago, and touched his forehead so gently, with a sweet blessing. From that day on, I knew he would be ok. That, I will never forget."

Earle Simmons said: "As a young man, I remember being struck by Miss Ruth's kindness, her wisdom and her sense of propriety. Her teachings transcended the Sunday School classroom at St. Paul's; and from her we learned about life, family and community. She encouraged us to seek answers, understanding and truth on our own terms. Ms. Kinnard was a teacher, a mentor, a storyteller, a lady and above all, a dear friend, whose memory will forever touch anyone who has had the pleasure of knowing her. She opened up our minds and let us into her heart."

In 2004, Ruth Kinnard's association and devotion to St. Paul's were memorialized by her daughter with a beautiful, stained-glass, front window with an image of St. Michael – a favorite of Ms. Ruth's. When one sees the sun shine through this window from the inside of the church, its bright and colorful array can only recall Ms. Ruth's love of life, beauty and the importance of knowledge that came from her and her activities in Franklin's St. Paul's Episcopal Church.

Alyne Massey

My thoughts of Ruth Kinnard go back so many years. I was sorry that after I left Franklin I did not see her very often. However, I read about her and was so very proud of her work with the judiciary.

I knew Ruth when she was a young mother and wife. Her husband was handsome and successful and her children were wonderful. She had a special way with children and I remember when Bill and Bob would go to Martlesham Heath and come home raving about a special treat. She would serve them toast covered with butter and jelly then put under the broiler. All of this with a big mug of hot chocolate!

When time passed and circumstances changed, Ruth adapted with great aplomb. She was strong and smart and a natural leader – a Tri Delta sorority sister who mentored many young people in the right direction.

Alyne

Carol McCoy

My first recollection of Ruth Kinnard was during my first year at Vanderbilt Law School in 1970-71 when Martha Johnson, now Martha Trammel, introduced us. Ruth was a stunning, elegant lady who had finished Vanderbilt Law School a few years earlier and was practicing at that time. She was beautifully coiffed, and spoke with an enticing, breathless voice that made you always hunger for the next word or phrase that she was going to speak. She made me realize that practicing law did not mean that you had to abandon one's manners or grace.

Within a short time after I met her, Ruth became a U.S. Bankruptcy Judge and her picture was put in the newspaper, again reflecting the elegance that typified Ruth's appearance. She customarily wore a solid gold cross on a large chain around her neck during the latter years of her life – she found comfort in her faith and in practicing her faith on a daily basis.

In the courtroom, Ruth was dignified and precise. She was courteous to the attorneys and the litigants and when necessary, could ask cogent and pointed questions. She was very aware of the circumstances that brought the individuals to her specialized court – financial hardship had been a brief, but personal experience for Ruth after her husband died. She recounted how a trust had been established by her late husband, but not well managed. As a consequence, Ruth realized that she was going to have to provide for herself if she desired to maintain her same lifestyle – and with a strong inner drive and determination, she sought the law.

As I reflect upon Ruth's life, I find that her faith and her profession

– both based on very basic tenets – the Golden Rule and the law of contracts – were of utmost importance to her. She observed them both and used them both, to benefit all she knew. A wonderful lady throughout her life, Ruth dedicated her talents, intellect and charm to help many others improve their lives. She left a wonderful legacy of good works, framed in our memory by the harmony and southern gentility that she exemplified.

Gilbert Merritt

Ruth Kinnard first became my law clerk in 1967 when I was U.S. District Attorney and then became my friend, confidante and advisor. She became the good friend of my wife, Louise Fort Merritt, when we moved to Franklin in 1970 and became her neighbor. Thereafter, she became a mentor for my children – Stroud, Louise Clark and Eli – as they were growing up in Franklin. She taught their Sunday School classes at St. Paul's and had a major impact on our lives for many years. When my wife died in 1973, Ruth went to Disneyland with us after her funeral where we began the process of adjustment and healing that gradually takes place in the face of such a life-shattering event. All of us turned to her many times over the next twenty-five years.

Ruth had a tender soul and believed devoutly that she was sent here to follow the teachings of Christ to be a good Samaritan. She came as close to that ideal as human nature permits. She never passed a brother or sister by.

She was in law school when she applied to be a summer clerk. Her letter said she was from Franklin and listed her educational background and a few other facts like having been the President of the national Tri-Delts. I walked down the hall to Frank Gray's chambers to ask if he knew her. He said, "Yes," and that he had suggested that she apply for the clerkship job. He said you will always be glad you hired her because she is a "remarkable woman." That was an understatement.

I think she cared so much because she herself had suffered through many tragic moments and had an empathy and love that passes understanding and explanation. Her heart radiated the Holy

Spirit that she taught so many children, including Stroud, Clark and Eli, to believe in and listen for. In my mind's eye, I still see her smiling face and the long golden cross that she often wore. I can see her as she embraced each one of us as we met and parted and made each feel that we were her special friend. She had that special grace and graciousness, so rare and extraordinary. Her memory still brings joy to the hearts of all who knew her.

Jane Montague

As I remember Ruth Kinnard, I think – talented, intelligent, wise, generous, hospitable.

Jane Montague

Beth & Rusty Moore
Law Partners and Friends

Ruth Kinnard is one of the world's great souls – a servant after whom we can all hope to pattern our lives. She met each and every day with an infectious joy and each relationship with a rare sincerity. She welcomed every person with love and a caring spirit. Her law practice brought her together with those on top of the world and those who felt they had hit the bottom. Yet, she made a strong lasting connection with all that she met and had a message for everyone. Her life was a lesson in grace and compassion. Her long life, well lived, strengthened by faith, was a gift that lives on in the many that she influenced.

For two young lawyers at Stokes & Bartholomew, Ruth was a friend and mentor. A woman with strength of character who helped guide us through professional and personal situations. She was brilliant and incredibly insightful. Ruth shared with us some of the most joyous moments of our lives and held our hands in the darkest times we have experienced. Amazingly, she always had the right words and a presence of joy, love and comfort.

We have all loved the notes and letters that seemed to always appear at the perfect time. We have included one that is so Ruth Kinnard and to which many can probably relate. When our son Roe was baptized, Ruth gave him the gift of a beautiful hand made woman's handkerchief. The beautiful note she included instructs that the handkerchief is a gift for Roe to present to his bride on his wedding day. A few years later, she wrote a beautiful letter to our daughter Ellie at her baptism and presented another beautiful handkerchief for her wedding. Think about that, what a special gift…

simple, elegant, touching.

One of our family's most meaningful traditions began with a letter from Ruth to our son. When Roe was three, Ruth wrote a letter of instruction to him on how to make an Advent wreath from fresh greenery and encouraged us to set aside a time each Sunday to light the candle, read scripture and pray. Our Advent wreath and candle lighting ritual is now an important part of our holiday season and one that we enjoy sharing with family and friends.

Ruth's heart was always open. She was the go to person – always willing to offer her support and never needing attention or recognition in return. Ruth had so many accomplishments in her life and career that are truly incredible. But, above all those wonderful successes, Ruth walked with God in her daily life. Her daily life was a profession of her faith without judgment of others. She influenced by example. Her influence was powerful. It lives on today when any of us write a sincere note, give a meaningful gift or comfort a friend.

We look forward to the time when our children are married and the letters from Ruth are presented to them. It will be wonderful for us to tell them about Ruth Kinnard. It will be another occasion to be reminded of the many acts of kindness shown to us by a remarkable person. Our lives are so much better from having known this beautiful soul.

12-13-96
Dear Roe,

I know you like to do projects with your father and this is one I think you will enjoy each year. It is to make an Advent wreath with four purple or navy blue candles and one white one in the middle.

Advent is the season of the Christian year which are the four Sundays before Christmas. Put the four blue candles on a tray in a circle with the white candle in the center. Put the oasis in the circle between the candles and fill the oasis with snippets of greens from your garden. Each Sunday you light a blue/purple candle, read something from the Bible and say a prayer. The next Sunday you light two, then three, then four and finally on Christmas you light the white candle.

Because I am late in suggesting this to you, you would need to light three purple candles on December 15 then all four on December 22.

You do not have to be catholic to have an Advent wreath. I think more and more churches are observing the seasons of the Christian year. Anna Russell Thornton has an Advent wreath. The kitchen table — where you have breakfast — is a good place to keep your wreath.

Advent is a penitential season when we prepare our hearts for the coming of Jesus.

If you are worn out with projects, put these away until next year.

> *Love, Love.*
> *Ruthie*

Agnes Fort More

When I took pen in hand in an effort to put into words my thoughts of that most unique and awesome and inspiring individual, Ruth Kinnard, I began by looking back upon the excellent people it has been my good fortune to know in my 71 years. After much scrutiny, I conclude that rarely, if ever, have I known the equal of Ruth Kinnard. Raised in Alabama (and she was very proud of that!) Ruth's "way of going" could be termed (and you will be surprised at this nomenclature): Southern Belle. Belle according to Webster's meaning: "n., a popular and attractive girl or woman whose charm and beauty made her a favorite." (Let it be said here: the word "belle" is not to be confused, as it often is, with a girl or woman, described as superficial, selfish, helpless and trite with a Southern drawl.)

This Southern Belle/Ruth Kinnard full of grace, a favorite of many, carried on the true Southern tradition of Womanhood – not only a "belle" but a devoted and tireless matriarch and homemaker, a determined leader, a good Samaritan, a fine Christian woman active in every aspect of her church; a woman struggling with and surviving life's griefs and adversities, made more content, more productive with each setback; a wise counselor, an attentive listener, a memorable teacher; honest, intelligent, trust-worthy; loved and loving; a woman who had friends in all generations; a friend to persons of diversified creeds and interests.

In a word, Ruth Kinnard was a woman of excellence.

A favorite Ruth Kinnard was!

A favorite Ruth Kinnard remains today to all those who take

joy in her remembrance. I leave it to others to describe the specifics of her involvement in her family, in her community and in her profession. Her achievements therein are legion and legendary.

In this world we live in: Today more than ever, we revere, we miss and we yearn for the sort of mentor and friend that Ruth Kinnard was to all who crossed her path.

Ruth Kinnard lives on in our hearts and we have been blessed in knowing her.

George Paine

Friend, Mother, Fellow Episcopalian, Mentor/mentee, Judge and Lawyer Connections

Of everyone I have known Ruth Kinnard would be the hardest to pigeon hole as to what our relationship was. However the easy part of this is what she meant to me and everyone else who came in contact with her.

I first knew Ruth as Mrs. Kinnard when I was a boarding student at BGA, an experience no worse than any POW has experienced in any of our wars. In addition to friends that made the school and Franklin tolerable were persons like Ruth who were few and far between. Not only was her home always open to us but she was so wonderful it was as if she wasn't a mother but a friend who never spoke down to you but as equal. It also helped that she knew everyone in the world so the mention of your grandmother would bring instant recognition (in my case it was a Tri Delta connection).

Later on when our relationship was transformed to one of a treasured friend I told her how awful we found Franklin and our existence at BGA. In response she said she always chaffed under the small town atmosphere and longed for a larger world with more intellectual ferment. It wasn't that she didn't enjoy Franklin but she, like us, yearned for far more exotic surroundings. And I had always thought it was a thought exclusive to us. This needless to say had a huge impact on me, especially that she was willing to share it with me.

Part of our friendship was hers with my wife, Ophelia, and our two boys, Carter and Thompson. Christmas wasn't complete without the boys' personalized tree ornaments that they still put up on our tree each year. One of the most wonderful things about that annual tradition of Ruth's is that I discovered that my boys had the same feelings toward Ruth that I did. She truly transcended age and the generations better than any person I have known.

Along with our friendship we also shared a wonderful professional relationship that morphed over the years.

She went back to law school late in life, and it was inspiring to all of us who were going to or thinking about going to law school or getting our experience interrupted by the draft. We all realized that if Ruth could do it at her age, our experience would be de minimis compared to hers.

We then had a relationship as a judge with me as the lawyer. It was great fun to practice before her and, without knowing it at the time, she was modeling for me when I too became a judge in her court. It made my ascendancy to the bench all the more meaningful because she had been there before me.

Also in this legal relationship I had the pleasure of practicing law with her which was a complete joy. Not only could I hang out with her as a friend, but I could also call on her whenever I had a legal problem that needed her legal guidance and nurturing. She was one of the unique senior lawyers for whom no question is too dumb or obvious when of course it was. However she never let on that it was and protected your self esteem and ego (not that male lawyers are bothered with either).

Although it was all too fleeting, I did have the pleasure of occasional appearances by her in my court. Never did any client have a more long suffering and empathetic lawyer than Ruth. She helped people others had completely avoided or long ago given up on. But that was Ruth, and it never surprised us.

Lastly I knew Ruth as the ultimate Episcopalian. Although I grew up as a Methodist and like to say Sewanee made the (True and Perfect) church irresistible it was actually role models like Ruth from my earliest days at BGA and at St Paul's who played a large part of this process. After I joined and became active in Christ Church in

Nashville, I realized that all of us should live our lives the way Ruth did on a daily basis in church and out of it.

Ophelia would echo all of this (with the exception of the BGA incarceration), and Ruth was a dear friend to her as well as me. I can't believe she's gone, but not really because she truly does live on in each of us because of the way she touched our lives.

Mary Pearce

Ruth Kinnard, Friend, Mentor and President of the Heritage Foundation of Franklin and Williamson County.

Ruth was greatly interested in the Heritage Foundation and preserving Franklin's rich architectural history. At the time she became President, I was a fairly new executive director, and she urged me to be professional, fair, and understanding of the business and development community. She was always interested in Franklin, learning from leading preservationists. We invited them to Franklin and they came – everyone from William Cecil, owner of Biltmore, to the President of the National Trust. When Mr. Cecil visited Franklin, she hosted a luncheon at Belle Meade Country Club. As an alderman and preservationist, she led the effort to gain approval for historic overlay zoning to protect historic resources in our community. When she was president of the Heritage Foundation, she told me she didn't care how many hours I worked, "Just get the job done." I think those who knew Ruth can hear her saying it. During her two years as president, we nominated over 130 properties to the National Register of Historic Places. She was a mentor to me by an act as simple as giving me a portfolio holder to carry to meetings after seeing me show up with a notebook. She was always quick to praise and offered gentle, thoughtful advice. Ruth had an ability to make us at the Heritage Foundation feel very valued by remembering the staff at Christmas and praising us in public. I saw her as a wonderful role model and when making decisions relating to work, I still ask myself, "would Ruth approve?" When I had her support, I knew I was on the "right track" and could always count on a hand written note applauding my work and ending with "Cheers, Ruth." As a friend, she was interested in my children, Holly and Stephen, who were friends with her grandchildren, Brandon and Clay. She was the most elegant and engaging lady in Franklin and made everything interesting and exciting. She could make a visit to Merridees a grand adventure, and her small home on Evans Street was as stylish as her loft apartment on Main Street. On more than one occasion, I met with her in the apartment at 4th and Main. She would "hold court" in a silk slip, smoking a cigarette and offering advice on the topic of the day. She had such a sparkle and great style. On the day Ruth passed away, she had made plans to come to the Annual Meeting of the Heritage Foundation she helped found, to be honored along with her long time friend and fellow preservationist, Sue Berry. We were very saddened and shocked to learn Ruth had passed away on the day we planned to salute her work. Both ladies were receiving the only Preservation Legacy Awards the Heritage Foundation has ever presented. This award was created to honor two citizens who were key to the historic preservation work in Franklin and Williamson County. Ruth knew she was getting the award, and I know that in her very critical but fair way of thinking, knew she had earned this distinction. I know for a fact that she wanted to be remembered for her leadership in protecting the rich heritage of her community. You ask how I know? Well, on a very cold winter day about a year or so before she died, Sue and Ruth arranged a conference call with me. Both ladies, who were never ones to "toot their own horns," were concerned that the history of the preservation movement in Franklin would be written without their being recognized as playing a role in what was their passion and volunteer effort for many years. I assured them I would do my part in making sure "the record showed" what they had done. Eunetta Kready, Danny Anderson, and I took the idea of the Heritage Legacy Award to the board of directors of the Heritage Foundation, and the idea was approved that this distinction go to these two deserving women. I consider the opportunity to have worked with her, be supervised by her, and just to know her, a blessing.

I miss her sparkle. It is always fun to run into Jon Kinnard and chat with him, and for a few minutes, enjoy the wonderful laugh he inherited from Ruth – Cheers, to you Ruth!

Mary Pearce

Bert Phillips

History changed on October 4, 1957, when the Soviet Union successfully launched Sputnik. The world's first satellite was about the size of a basketball, weighed only 183 pounds, and took 98 minutes to orbit the Earth. News of this momentous event interrupted "Shock Theatre" that we – Judy's friends, and I was a new one, and this is my first clear memory of being around Ruth – were watching on the big television under Clay's "Ace" portrait in the Kinnards' front den at Martlesham Heath.

The timing of this was an omen for me, for as time would tell, there was usually something auspicious and profound going on around Ruth. I associate her with our desire to get out of here and into Heaven.

Ruth left me with no articulated wisdom. Rather, it was a feeling of having had intimacy with an old soul. There is a Sanskrit word for this, "darsan" – the glow one acquires through resonance, by being in the company of a Master.

Initially we connected through books. Ruth turned me on to James Agee's *Letters to Father Flye*. What a strange and delicious experience. Remember, I went to Battle Ground Academy, where everything was yea team, football, and a Billy Graham sort of notion of Christianity. They didn't make 'em like Ruth where I was coming from, not in those days.

For some curious reason my Ruth brain cells are near those attached to Winston Churchill. There was, I don't know . . . that vibe, that spirit. A heavy noble warmth of soul. Passion, pragmatism. And sometimes, depression. Though doubtless Ruth was aided a bit by Tareytons and scotch, I think by choice she came to Earth too soon for the SRIs. She dealt with inner darkness on her own. And she was a model for how to do it.

Ruth was not literally my God Mother, but she might as well have been. The Episcopal Church joined us. We both groped with Faith. Often I sought her counsel.

And in the everyday grown-up world I sought Ruth's company over lunch – at Rotiers, Irelands, the Belle Meade Motel, at the kinda sorta nice place on Main Street in Franklin. Downtown, in her lawyer years, we ate at the uptight Cumberland Club (conveniently located in her building) where everyone knew her and, better, also where everyone knew her, Satsuma.

Ruth never ate very much. Her hunger was more arcane.

After the passing of Suzuki Roshi, the man who founded the first Zen Centers in America, his disciples posited that the horrible death he experienced, ravaged by cancer, indicated that this was his last round, that his spirit was burning off the final dross of earthly existence. And though Ruth would doubtless claim she needed to go around a few more times, still, I think of her death this way. And Clay's, too. Maybe this was a part of some joint venture.

The last time I saw Ruth she put me in mind of the little old lady from "Babar," thin, tiny even, with great personal style, dressed in Parisian black. Ruth was so small! I was shocked.

It was Easter. By this time I lived in Colorado and Ruth lived in her little house. Our plan was early Communion at Saint Paul's, then breakfast.

It was too early for the spot on Main Street and some unreliable source had suggested to her a new place off Highway 96 in what – to her chagrin – turned out to be a strip mall. The restaurant was one of those ubiquitous nowhere "Southern" joints representative of the New Franklin, just off the Interstate. But Ruth didn't feel particularly well and so rather than look for another spot we went inside. All around us were Junkteak Stores and next door, if you get the picture, was the Grace Christian All Souls Hair Salon and Weight Loss Center.

We ate quietly. So strange…to be creatures from a lost world. Neither of us recognized anybody in the restaurant. For Ruth, it was time, literally and metaphorically, to get out of Franklin, to get out of Tennessee, and to leave Mother Earth.

Ruth in Heaven:

> that monster gold cross
> weightless in a summer sky
> hulahoops her neck.

Bert Phillips

Sally Poe and Betty Astleford

We became close to Ruth near her retirement. She became a part of our family. We had lost a sister, and told her we were adopting her as our sister!

We enjoyed outings together – like driving back roads, especially enjoying portions of the Natchez Trace Parkway to see the deer. Eating out and eating in. Most importantly of all, we frequently had our Monday morning lunches on Sally's back porch! We referred to that as our "soul food lunches!" Enjoying hot water corn bread, black eye peas, fresh cream style corn, green beans, fresh tomatoes, cucumbers, squash, turnip greens, fried chicken! Friends were lucky to be invited to join us! Joining us most Mondays were Mary Amos and Christean Stearns who worked with Sally.

We marveled as to how diverse her friends were, from old to young. We could understand this as Ruth had such an interesting life and was a joy to be around. Very few people knew just how many people Ruth quietly helped.

Sally felt honored to have been able to host Ruth's 80th birthday celebration – which was such a great time with many people coming to honor her.

We have missed Ruth very much and continue to speak of her often. We are grateful to have had her touch our lives, and will continue to hold her memory close in our hearts!

Sally C. Poe
Betty (Astleford)

Jennifer Rawlings

I didn't meet Ruth until later in her life – and mine. We met on a Christmas morning at the Beasley's house. I don't remember exactly how we were introduced, but I vividly remember that I was instantly enamored with her and by the time David and I left to travel back to Nashville, both of us felt like we had made a friend in Ruth Kinnard.

Of course, I had heard about Ruth for years because of her close relationship with Allison and John and their children. I knew about her entering Vanderbilt Law School after her husband died and raising her children and practicing law. Now I had met the lady herself, and I was in awe of her graciousness to someone she had never laid eyes on. I was under her spell from that morning on.

When I really got to know and love Ruth was on a trip to Maine. David and I were invited to visit Allison and John at the same time that Ruth was invited. I remember so well walking through the front door, weary from the road, and here was this small woman sitting on the hearth with a cigarette in one hand and a drink in the other, and I knew we had come to the right place at the right time!

There are so many stories from that trip, but suffice it to say that David and I bonded with Ruth and felt like we had a friend for life. One day the Beasley's next door neighbor, Billy, took Ruth, David and me in a little (really little) boat out into the ocean. Ruth sat in the front holding on to both sides of the boat for dear life because (as we learned later) Billy took us farther out than we probably should have gone, but he had three landlocked Nashvillians that were

113

whooping and hollering and having such a grand time that he gave us our money's worth! I will never forget that special day with Billy at the helm and Ruth in her life jacket at the bow heading out to sea!

Ruth was a lady in every sense of the word. She had such warmth. She could make you feel that everything you said to her was so interesting when all along it was she that was the interesting half of the conversation. What a gift she had. What a gift she was to so many. She will always be missed…but never forgotten.

Jennifer Jawlings

Barbara King Rice

There are countless, deeply cherished, memories of Ruth. Her great source of knowledge and wisdom she graciously shared, those deep blue eyes that could see right into your soul, the way she effortlessly glided into a room always wearing her gold cross and her many gold bracelets; just like a movie star from an old movie with satin gowns and French telephones and ivory cigarette holders, the way she understood every single thing you felt that made you love her and be drawn to her and...that voice. Especially the voice. Ruth always called me "Tandy's Barbara" and was also the first person to ever call me "Mrs. Rice." She performed our wedding ceremony and later told my parents she "tied the knot 7 different ways!" Ruth told me I was exactly what Tandy had always needed and that she was grateful I was finally in his life.

I began to know Ruth when Tandy and I started seeing each other and I knew he adored her by the way his eyes always sparkled when he spoke of her. He often escorted her to social functions and I would tag along for the shear privilege of sharing time with Ruth and just to watch her. She was everything a woman should be. She was glorious and I loved to see her inter-act with people. We would often pack a picnic basket and have our picnic right there in Ruth's dining room. She once said she could live on good wine, cheese and bread and we always made sure the picnic included those items. I can shut my eyes and hear her voice. How did she always know the perfect words to say and did she know what a profound difference those words made in every life she touched? Ruth was like a miracle in life. A beautiful miracle.

A miracle that continues to smile in my heart.

Incidentally, that knot is still tied tighter than ever; just as she wanted it to be.

Barbara King Rice

Dave Richmond

TURNING LEMONS INTO LEMONADE

One of our fondest memories of Ms. Ruth was how she could always turn a troublesome time into something to be grateful for. In the early 1990's Franklin had some terrible storms that came through parts of Williamson County. We were either fortunate or misfortunate that the 'straight line' winds came into our property and went straight down our driveway snapping about 27 Bradford pear trees (almost 1 foot in base diameter) about 1-2 foot above the ground. Obviously they were all destroyed! I was outside with my tractor trying to tow the trees to a large burn pile. Several neighbors came by and expressed how terrible we must feel. Then Mrs. Ruth drove up in her car. I was obviously distressed, tired and sweat was rolling off my brow. Of course I expected her to say how bad she felt for the disaster. Her comment to me – was "Dave, you never liked these trees – isn't it nice you can now put in trees you really want!" Well, this advice will always stick with me in the future – she always had a way to take something terrible and turn it into something one can be grateful for!

I have often thought how great it is that when one walks into St. Paul's Church in Franklin, one enters through doors remade in her memory, a large stained glass window she gave in memory of her husband and another stained glass window given in her memory.

What a lasting tribute.

Malli Hart Richmond

SOME OF MY THOUGHTS AS I REFLECT
ABOUT OUR BELOVED RUTHIE

Ruth Kinnard was a dear friend of my mother, Ann Hart. I had the fortunate privilege to know her and love her from a young age. One special memory is the confirmation class she taught at St. Paul's Church in Franklin. I look back on these earlier years with appreciation for all that she taught and passed on to many young people.

Another distinct and fond memory was my sixteenth birthday. It was a surprise party with a small group of dear friends, which included, of course, Jon Kinnard and Will Berry. I will never forget Ruth arriving to pick me up in a wonderful two-seat Mercedes! As we arrived at Martlesham Heath, I caught a glimpse of a few faces peeking from behind the curtains of the library window. Hence, I knew there was a surprise awaiting!

When Dave and I were married at St. Paul's in 1983, it was Ruth who presented us with the Eucharistic candles from the altar that she had saved following the ceremony that July evening. We still have them. It was so indicative of her character.

One Fall in more recent years, I had the fortune of filling a cancelled space on the annual New York theater trip. My mother invited me to go along with her and Ruth and their friend, Josephine Gurley. It was one of the most entertaining several days I have ever had! Enjoying great lunches or dinners before or after the shows. Squeezing in some shopping time was also on our agenda.

But, being with these three intellectually diverse ladies will be an imprint on my mind forever. How glad I am I accepted the invitation!

Over the years we enjoyed Ruth's company during holiday dinners or quieter occasions in our home. She added a very special ambience when she entered the room. Her calming demeanor and tone in her voice always mesmerized those around the room.

The one trait for me she exemplified was her faith. She maintained such strength of wisdom and character. She had the gift to connect with people. Regardless of one's background or age, Ruth could relate. Her accomplishments are so great. But her way of sharing her wisdom was truly a gift she gave to all of us whose lives she touched. Each one is unique to each of us. I would always see things clearer after a good "dose" of Mrs. Ruth. I dearly loved her and I miss her very much. I am so thankful to have been blessed by knowing her.

Malli Richmond

John Seigenthaler

She was a presence. You could not meet her without feeling it. It – that presence – sort of embraced you when you ran into her.

It could be at a huge party. Or a small gathering at her place. Or at the market. Or in the courthouse. Wherever you found her (or she found you) you felt that presence.

She was Different. Unique. Special. Engaging. Caring. Secure. And strong.

On many subjects she could be serious beyond belief. She knew how to lecture: brief sermonettes of wisdom delivered in that breathless voice, almost hoarse at times. Here it is, was her message. Take it or leave it. It sounded at times like a conversational prayer, even when she would drop in a cuss word. And most often she left you saying (to yourself): Amen!

She knew how to laugh. It was a hearty half-rumble accompanied by dancing lights in her eyes. The sound of it made you want to laugh with her, to share her mirth, her joy.

She also knew how to listen. That is a rare gift. She would listen me to death.

Most of all, Ruth Kinnard knew how to love. She loved her own. She loved my own. She loved God's own. And I loved her.

Robert Sewell

I am honored to be among those asked to comment on memories of Ruth Kinnard.

As to our relationship, there were actually two – first, as a child being a recipient of that generous hospitality (who can forget Willow Plunge!) and love; and secondly, as her urologist.

There were decades between those two periods of time. I don't think I even saw her in the interim; but when she came in to see me as a patient a few years ago, it was as though no time had lapsed at all – she still looked as I remembered her, and she still had that wonderful dignified Southern drawl.

One of the most vivid childhood memories of my relationship with Ruth – yes, I called her Ruth at that time, and to the best of my recollection she insisted on that – occurred when she and Judy and Wink had moved to the house off Lewisburg Avenue. I think they had a pool in the backyard, and the "in thing" for kids our age was peroxided hair. We were all 9-10 years of age, and the word was out that Mrs. Kinnard had the right formula. I'm sure our own parents didn't want to fool with the stuff – whether they condoned it or not I'm not sure – but I imagine Ruth called to get their permission. I recall Harry and Paul Guffee, Tom Minton, Sam Lee (he already had blonde-white hair), and I were there. There were probably others. I'm quite sure we looked plain funny after drying out in the sun, but I sure felt "cool," and a big part of that was because Ruth assured us we were cool. She was like that. She was pretty cool herself.

125

Duke Shackelford

Ruth was a mother, friend and confidante to me during my four years at Battle Ground Academy. She was especially warm and helpful my freshman and sophomore years when I was very lonely and homesick.

What a wonderful Southern Lady! Ruth had the unique ability to make everyone around her feel so very special.

I will forever be grateful and indebted to Ruth, Judy and all the Kinnards for helping make my years at BGA a *very, very* special time in my life. *God Bless Ruth Kinnard.*

Duke

Michael Sheridan

LESSONS ACROSS GENERATIONS

Providence smiled on me the day Ruth Kinnard moved into the office next to mine at the law firm. Taken by her charms and hoping to secure her companionship, I quickly purchased an ashtray for my office, though I myself did not smoke. I lucked out – Judge Kinnard found my ashtray useful and became a frequent and favored guest to my office.

Like so many, my admiration for Ruth Kinnard was immediate. Her genuine concern for others and willingness to share her experiences with a young lawyer were enriching. She was a teacher, teaching lessons across generations.

Judge Kinnard led a wonderful, full life. And she easily shared her life with others. This life, and her memories of it, were reflected in the people and objects that always surrounded her. People like John Beasley, Judge Koch and Tandy Rice. Objects like the portrait of a gallant Colonel Clay Kinnard, still wearing his Mae West keeping vigil on a World War II airfield awaiting the safe return of his squadron from a mission. Then too, there were her copies of Thomas Wolfe's novels, including her favorite, *Look Homeward Angel*. And, of course, there were the ubiquitous Salvatore Ferragamo shoes. Ruth's charms were such that many of us learned a little something from all of these people and things – even her shoes.

Ruth was 21 years old and a senior at the University of Alabama when she first read Thomas Wolfe's *Look Homeward Angel*. Wolfe's editor was Maxwell E. Perkins, who was employed at

Charles Scribner's Sons in the 1920s and 1930s. In addition to Wolfe, Ernest Hemingway and Scott Fitzgerald were the most prominent writers with whom he worked. For Fitzgerald, Perkins played many roles, chief among which was lender to support a lifestyle and image that Fitzgerald's income from writing often failed to sustain. Max Perkins also served as somewhat of a psychoanalytical counselor for Fitzgerald, and, I suspect, the other writers with whom he worked, including Thomas Wolfe with whom, as Ruth told me, she was "besotted."

As a young woman, Ruth had an occasion to be in New York City. In advance of her trip, she wrote to Max Perkins, hoping to correspond with Thomas Wolfe or, if at all possible, meet Mr. Wolfe during her New York trip. She was shocked to actually receive a reply from Perkins. Perkins conveyed that he was unable to arrange a meeting between Ruth and Mr. Wolfe, but that Perkins would be honored to meet Ruth for cocktails during her visit.

So, Ruth and Max Perkins shared an afternoon having cocktails at the Algonquin Hotel on West 44th Street in midtown Manhattan, just around the corner from the Charles Scribner offices on Fifth Avenue. Perkins told Judge Kinnard intimate accounts of the lives of some of America's greatest fiction writers. Of how Fitzgerald actually discovered Hemingway in Paris, bringing him to the attention of Charles Scribner's Sons. Forty years later, Ruth shared some of these stories with me, teaching me more about these writers and imparting a greater love for their works. Fitzgerald's *Tender Is The Night* was first published in April 1934, the same month as Ruth's birthday. Every spring, I reread *Tender Is The Night* and am reminded of Ruth's afternoon with Max Perkins.

Judge Kinnard's last home was a cottage in Franklin, Tennessee which she named Saffron Walden after an old town south of Cambridge, England where Clay Kinnard was stationed for a time during World War II. Visitors to Ruth's Saffron Walden will recall seeing a stone angel in her front garden. From Thomas Wolfe, Ruth had desired the "soft stone smile of an angel." On her 79th birthday, Ruth got her stone angel from a shopkeeper on Nolensville

Road in Nashville. Spanning fifty-eight years, Ruth's connection with Thomas Wolfe had led her from Max Perkins and midtown Manhattan to a nameless shopkeeper in Nashville, and culminated in the delivery of a special birthday gift that, as she wrote, "guards over my cottage and tries to keep me happy."

Ruth's first job after graduating from the University of Alabama was with the Delta Delta Delta sorority as its Traveling National Secretary. I do not pretend to know what important responsibilities were vested with the Traveling National Secretary, but Ruth did tell me that this employment afforded her the opportunity to go to Chicago, home of some center of power for the Tri-Delts.

Today, walking along Chicago's "Magnificent Mile," one will come across the Salvatore Ferragamo boutique on Michigan Avenue. For as long as I knew her, Judge Kinnard always wore nothing but low Salvatore Ferragamo pumps with grosgrain bows. These shoes are expensive, impeccable and, I think, a symbol of Ruth's consistency. In a way, a tribute to her loyalty and appreciation for a limited number of fine, material things in life. She would tell all of us to enjoy something in the way she enjoyed her Ferragamo shoes. I wonder whether her love for these shoes was first born during her time in Chicago working hard for Tri-Delt.

In 1998, Ruth and I met for lunch in Franklin to discuss a project. She was wearing a brand-new pair of beautiful eggshell white Ferragamos – her trademark. I had been honored because she had just opened the shoebox, exclusively for our lunch.

I came to appreciate Ruth's consistency in footwear selection for at least three reasons. First, in today's world where nothing is constant or remains the same, it was both refreshing and reassuring to have found someone like Ruth Kinnard – a former Federal government official – who was consistent about anything, even shoes. It was from this perspective that I perhaps learned something important by comparing Ruth and her loyalty to Salvatore Ferragamo with any government official today on any subject, including shoes. Today's citizenry knows all too well that present day politicians and government officials – be they Republican, Democrat or

Independent – have absolutely no consistent stand on anything, including something as seemingly simple as shoes. With Ferragamo, Ruth was, perhaps, telling us that in order to take a stand one must have their feet firmly planted somewhere, hopefully in meaningful values and beliefs. In some way, perhaps Salvatore Ferragamo shoes helped Ruth keep her feet firmly planted, removing all doubt about where she stood. From her shoes, Ruth taught me something of consistency and loyalty.

Second, one should appreciate Ruth's wearing of Ferragamo shoes simply because she loved Ferragamo shoes. In Fitzgerald's *Tender Is The Night*, Nicole Diver insists that Rosemary's mother take Nicole's yellow evening bag, saying, "I think things ought to belong to the people that like them." The recognition that people are, in some way, comforted by those who are in possession of objects they love (e.g., a stone garden angel or Ferragamo shoes) is a theme occurring everyday, though we may not recognize it. I was comforted by the fact that Ruth had her Ferragamos, just as Nicole Diver was comforted by the fact that Rosemary's mother now had a yellow evening bag. Perhaps it is no coincidence that both Colonel Clay Kinnard and Scott Fitzgerald were both stationed at Maxwell Field, Alabama and fell in love with natives of Montgomery, Alabama – Ruth and Zelda.

Third and last, one should have appreciated Ruth's insistence on Salvatore Ferragamo because it was a marriage of beauty. Judge Kinnard was beautiful in many ways and it was only fitting that she be shod in beautiful shoes. Ferragamo put a finishing touch on the beauty, sophistication and goodness that was our Ruth. And for that, we owe Salvatore Ferragamo our thanks.

Michael W. Sheridan

Su Su Silva

I was lucky enough to have lived in Franklin in the 1950's when it was a real, Southern small town where everyone knew each other, and there were no subdivisions branching out all over the county on any land that wasn't a Harpeth River flood plain. I wasn't a native, having moved there when I was eleven, but I realized pretty soon that Mrs. Clay Kinnard, Miss Ruth, was the Queen of Franklin. She presided over St. Paul's Episcopal where I was in her Sunday school class. She seemed to always be at the family-owned Willow Plunge pool, the center of summer life for so many kids, making sure that all was running properly. However, I think my most memorable moments were equestrian ones. I took English riding lessons from Mrs. Cynthia Schell as did so many in that era including Ruth's daughter, Judy. We would mount our horses at the stable behind Dr. Fred Schell's horse vet clinic on Columbia Pike, go clip-clopping and often sliding down the road, cross over the railroad tracks, through a creek and onto the beautiful Kinnard farm where we would practice our horsemanship, jumping, and get tossed now and then. I broke my leg when I was fourteen when my pony refused a jump. Ruth's support of riding events and the Schells enabled many of us of that era to participate in horse shows, fox hunting, and the start of one of the first Pony Clubs in the U.S. I still have a few rather tarnished silver cups but nothing like Judy Kinnard who won so many trophies her mother had to build a little cabinet to display them all. Ruth did many things for many people, a reason why she was such a respected and admired woman. When the Schells left Franklin so Dr. Schell could teach at Auburn, and I no longer had their horses to ride, it appeared to be the end of my riding since I couldn't afford to own one. Miss Ruth came to my rescue and let me ride her son Wink's pony and compete in shows on him for a few years until my family moved away to Nashville. A small example of her generosity, but it meant a lot to me.

Ruth Kinnard was a stellar example of what a woman could achieve to many young girls of that pre-Feminist era – wife and mother to three, a pillar of the religious community, a mover and shaker, and a law degree in mid-life! She was the Queen of Franklin.

Su Su Silva

Eric Skinner

Many images come to mind growing up Episcopalian in Franklin, Tennessee, in the 1960s and 70s. Dark wood. Light-streaming stained glass. Red naugahide kneelers. Few images though are more powerful and speak to Christian commitment and responsibility than the living icon sitting in the second pew from the front, Epistle side of the sanctuary. First seat, center aisle. Judge Ruth Kinnard sat there every week of my young church life.

What made Judge Kinnard any different from any of the 100 or so worshipers on Sunday morning? She sat alone; she sat with God, seemingly having a personal seat in the presence of the Divine. We little children were mesmerized by the enormous gold cross that hung from her neck, its weight seemingly pulling her forward in her reverential posture. At a very young age, the children at St. Paul's Episcopal Church recognized that the solitary figure seated in the second pew was a Christian, a spiritual traveler whose vehicle was prayer and obedience.

As St. Peter is the rock of Christ's church and ministry, Judge Kinnard was for us at St. Paul's, His stately marble pillar. Early on I recall watching this woman with whom I didn't share an intimate relationship—she was one of my parents' elders—seated in that pew. From toddler to fifth grade, we didn't know her other than through her presence in that seat and through the awkward adult/child pleasantries swapped in fellowship hall following the service. My two brothers and I shook her hand firmly each week, made respectful eye contact (lest my father made another type of eye contact with us) and said, "It's nice to see you, Judge Kinnard."

However, as a sixth grader, I did know Judge Kinnard. As sixth graders, my brothers knew Judge Kinnard, as every Episcopalian kid in Franklin was newly acquainted to her. At St. Paul's, sixth graders did not participate in Confirmation Class, we were members of Judge Kinnard's Confirmation Class. The class was the first rite of passage many of us experienced—looming, intimidating, even dreaded by some. I remember my brilliant, over-achieving older brother, Chip, visibly nervous as a boy entering Judge Kinnard's Confirmation Class. I also clearly recall Chip leaving her class as a young Christian man.

We Episcopalian sixth graders learned what it meant to take our faith seriously, to commit to memory the creeds and ancient prayers, to accept Christ's love and membership in His church. We learned about respect and decorum. We learned to sit still and to be accountable for the choices we made. We learned about sacred space. We learned what had been going on in the second row, first seat, center aisle all these years and that if her gold cross had, in fact, pulled Judge Kinnard forward, it was a joyous burden that she accepted in obedience to her Lord.

Nearly 30 years after completing Judge Kinnard's Confirmation Class, I don't remember much of the theology of the Church or of the policy that made us Episcopalians or even much about the specific teachings of Christ that we learned in the class. I do recall a firm but gentle and loving hand, the hand inspired by the One who called her to teach the sixth graders.

The last time I saw Judge Kinnard was at a family celebration of my 24th birthday at the Nashville City Club. I had recently graduated from college and had accepted my first job. My already-successful brother, Chip, hosted the event. I recall Judge Kinnard walking directly to our table and directly to me, a scene that would have rattled me as a sixth grader. After a firm handshake and then an even more firm embrace, she said simply, "Hello, Eric. I am proud of you."

This busy woman made time and interest to follow my life. From my paralyzing spinal cord injury and physical rehabilitation, to success in school and the beginning of a career. "Hello, Eric. I am proud of you." As impressed as I was that she remembered me and knew my life somewhat intimately, I was more taken aback by the realization that Judge Ruth Kinnard had addressed a young Christian man – one of her young Christian men.

Paul Sloan

THE PRESENCE OF RUTH

As life ripens, its meaning often lifts from the fog of youth with surprising clarity. One's limitations become more agreeable, worth more easily discerned, and reflections more instructive. Transitions become less often marked by clear bright lines than noted in retrospect, with the sudden awareness that a passage has occurred.

These thoughts bring to mind Ruth Kinnard.

With aging, I've learned that the shape and form of life is very personal and keyed by reference to specific people. We thread their memory, in bits and pieces, into a quilt of meaning that comforts us and tells us who we are and how best to live our lives. Some are family, a few are friends, some mere acquaintances and others the gift of reading. We piece together elements of each into our own unique view of the world.

Ruth has been, for me, one of those defining people. Whether by serendipity or design, Ruth has been present during my important passages. She was my first Sunday school teacher at St. Paul's (though she should not be judged by the results of that effort). In my adolescence, she was among those few elders who "got it." Her home was the seat of many discussions that held fast our inquiring minds.

As a young man, I returned from England to enter first year of law school just as she was completing her last. A few years later, as I was cutting my teeth as a young lawyer, she became the first woman to be appointed to Tennessee's federal bench as bankruptcy judge for the Middle District. Arguing a client's case before a judge who had taught you the Lord's Prayer at age six is an occurrence that gives one perspective.

Twenty years later, Ruth celebrated the birth of my son, Paul, with the gift of a blanket, which became his favorite among all others. As I now write, Paul is six and still sleeps in the comfort of the worn, tattered remains of that blanket. The connectivity is of equal comfort to me.

The spirits of great souls survive their mortal captors. Of that I have no doubt. Through my sixty years, Ruth has always been present, engaged, and relevant. And now, unbeknownst to son Paul, she has become one of the pieces in the quilt that will some day provide him his own unique worldview. That makes me very happy.

Paul Alcorn

Shelley Snow

Ruth Kinnard was a steel magnolia. If others have described her in that trite way, it is because it is a true description. She was a lady in the finest southern tradition, genteel, with her broad southern accent. She was generous, and loving and stood with grace amidst any crowd in any place. She was also timeless, one that understood children and could make anyone feel at ease, no matter how much you spilled on her carpet. She once said to me when I was a child, "Children don't asked to be born, so we as parents, need to make your life as beautiful as we can." But she was also strong and much ahead of her time, strong and fearless as she showed everyone when her husband died and she went back to law school and became a judge. What a green beret; she was an amazing lady. I first met her when I was about five years old and we moved from west Texas to Franklin, Tennessee. My, oh My, what on earth did the Kinnards think of us? West Texas cowboys and cowgirls moving into Carnton with all their western ways and western saddles and western horses, cowboys going and coming, roping calves and riding wild horses and Brahma bulls? There was Ruth and her sweet bunch of children riding English and hosting pony club meetings. Ruth Kinnard never batted an eye, at least to us , she was as gracious as a peach on a summer day. We joined the pony club, Daddy put Judy on one of his quarter horses and she jumped him like he had been trained in Tidewater, Virginia, which was the name of her own horse at the time. About six months before Ruth died, I picked up the phone one night and called her. She was in a lot of pain. But we talked about our days at Carnton and Martlesham Heath and we both cried, because as she said, there were so many memories that she had not talked about in so long, or thought about, and we talked a long time that night. About two days later, I opened my mailbox and got a hand written note from her, saying how much that conversation had meant to her. That was Ruth, always trying to make you feel like you are so special. I loved her very much.

Susie Tyne

HOMAGE TO RUTH

I had the privilege of working for Ruth at Commerce Union Bank at the beginning of her career, and later, the pleasure of living near her for ten years. She had recently been widowed, and with one remaining child to educate and a farm to run, she decided to equip herself with a law degree from Vanderbilt Law School. From there, she arrived in the Trust Department.

For those who were fortunate enough to know her, she was a shining example of courage and determination as well as a person of substance. When I met her, her achievements were already legendary, and her life experience vast for one so relatively young. For the newly-fledged feminist graduates, she seemed a paragon of possibilities representing the best that women were capable of accomplishing. She had done it all, from marriage to children, to graduate school to career, and as I became better acquainted with her, I realized that she was an impossible act to follow.

When I imagine Ruth now, I see her throwing her head back, and I hear the ensuing burst of infectious laughter. Always quick to be amused and to amuse, she never failed to pass my desk without a smile and often stopped to whisper a funny tale guaranteed to delight. She sprinkled compliments liberally about the room as she made her way through the office, and even the most sullen did not fail to appreciate her warmth and good manners.

She dressed beautifully, with her skirts and blouses held in place by belts with splendidly molded buckles. As she walked, the large gold cross worn on a long chain around her neck would bump against the buckle and strike a mellow note which became rhythmic the further and faster she walked. I was always pleased to hear those Ruth sounds, the beat of the cross and the soft jingling of her bracelets. Life without her in the office was dreary.

As we came to know each other, she often told me about her children and life at Martlesham Heath, her interest in Franklin and historic preservation there, and her spiritual life which was centered and continually nurtured at St. Paul's. Her love of that church was profound, and her unshakeable Christian faith put into practice. Often I would hear her encouraging those who were feeling forlorn to come to the Heath, for it was a place of healing and peace and beauty. She recommended this cure to so many people that I had visions of her weekend lawns strewn with the emotionally wounded and her kitchen filled with fragile friends busily making pepper jelly, her other panacea for the temporary relief of misery. I knew that after a tiring week at work, many weekends would be spent listening to people's troubles and trying to help.

A part of this generous spirit was a desire to see all of her friends happy, and she believed that happiness and fulfillment for women was to be found in good marriages and in families. One of her winsome attributes was a decided penchant for matchmaking, and eventually she turned her attention to my future. I soon learned the lengths to which she was prepared to go when Cupid was invoked as she began to set in motion her desired conclusion of my spinsterhood.

Her choice was a young banker who had reason to visit the Trust Department from time to time and to consult with Ruth. Their business had nothing to do with me, but my attention was alerted one day when I overheard Ruth telling the young man not to thank her for the work she had done, that in fact, I had done it all. She said I had spent such long hours on their project that I must be exhausted and therefore deserved to be included in the invitation to lunch which he had just extended. Forced to invite me, these lunches went on to become regular occurrences. Feasting at Satsuma, the three of us would engage in congenial banter, and I would be thanked again for additional work I had not done.

Eventually, Ruth must have decided that it was time to change the pattern, and through her son, I was invited to the Heath for a Sunday supper to help him with his college selection. On the Friday morning before the appointed evening, the telephone on Ruth's desk rang. She jumped to answer it, and I watched in some amazement as she slumped down into the chair, swiveled her body around to face the wall and began to whisper inaudibly. Seconds after she replaced the receiver, my telephone rang, and it was the young banker. He got straight to the point and informed me that Ruth had invited him to dinner to discuss colleges and also had asked him to do her a favor. She was worried about me driving all the way to the Heath in the dark and wanted him to drive me, keeping her request their secret.

I am able to recall little about that Sunday night, mainly that we drank quantities of red wine out of glasses the size of fish bowls, ate by candlelight and never mentioned colleges. I imagine that we discussed the war in Vietnam, perhaps war in general, almost certainly James Agee and Father Flye, Tom Wolfe, and her adored Frank Sinatra. I think his music might have been playing in the background. Aspects of Christianity were always of great interest and were frequently topics of heated debate, and she never failed to mention her children of whom she was immensely proud. I remember that the conversations were especially lively, for I was not driven home and seen to my door until the early morning. The young banker invited me to have lunch with him later that day and dinner with him that night.

There have been and continue to be many consequences of that happy Sunday night supper at Martlesham Heath all those years ago. I married the banker and moved to Franklin, where Ruth's children became our close friends, and our children close friends of their children. Decades of love and devotion and enrichment continue, and we owe it all to Ruth, to her singular encouragement and dedication to each of us. She was a truly remarkable woman whose influence reached far beyond her ken and which continues to resound through all of us today. I like to think that Old Blue Eyes is serenading her now and forever. It's the very least she deserves.

Susan Tyne

Dudley West

I had a number of relationships with Ms. Kinnard during my lifetime.

I first knew her as the mom of my fellow kindergartner, Jon. She was always a close and respected family friend as I was growing up in Franklin. When I needed someone to write a recommendation for my Vanderbilt Law School application, she was happy to do so. After becoming a member of the bar, I came to know Ms. Kinnard as a respected colleague and was fortunate enough to have the opportunity to try a case with her as co-counsel. Needless to say, she provided a steadying hand and much sage advice.

In 1990, the Nashville Bar Association bestowed its highest award, the John C. Tune Public Service Award, upon Ms. Kinnard. I was an officer of the Association at the time and jumped at the opportunity to introduce her and to make the presentation.

As noted in the presentation, "it is pretty apparent that Judge Kinnard assumed many different roles in her life:

– a southern belle who married a war hero;

– a loving mother of three children, six grandchildren and at least sixteen godchildren;

– a pioneer among women in the legal profession and the Federal judiciary;

– a dedicated civic and government leader in both Nashville and Franklin."

My conclusion then, however, as now, is that if you had to use only one description of Ms. Kinnard, the most fitting would be that of a deeply caring and religious person.

Ms. Kinnard was one of those rare people blessed with the God-given ability to make every person with whom she came in contact feel better about themselves and the world in general after any visit with her. She was truly an elegant lady in every respect. It was an honor to have been her friend.

Presentation Of John C. Tune Public Service Award
December 6, 1990

The John C. Tune Public Service Award is the highest award bestowed by the Nashville Bar Association. This award was established in 1983 to be given to the NBA member who has shown the highest degree of dedication, not only to his or her work as a lawyer, but to the betterment of the community in which he or she lives. This award is not necessarily given annually, but only when there is someone deserving of it.

The first recipient was John C. Tune, a Nashville attorney and community leader who died of cancer in 1983, and for whom the award is named. In accepting the award on behalf of her husband a few years ago, I remember Mrs. Tune saying that John Tune learned "early on" the joys of giving. This year the Board has decided unanimously that there is someone deserving of this award, and like John Tune, she is someone who truly knows the joys of giving.

The lady we honor tonight, Judge Ruth Kinnard, is one of the most compassionate professionals in this Association – and perhaps the most beloved. Her entire life is a legacy of giving – giving to her family, to her profession, to her community, and to her church.

Judge Kinnard was born in Camden, Alabama, and in 1940 was a Phi Beta Kappa graduate of the University of Alabama. Upon graduation, after working as a reporter for a Montgomery newspaper, she served as a traveling secretary of her college sorority, Tri-Delta, later becoming its national president. During World War II she married Claiborne Kinnard, an Air Force fighter pilot then stationed in Montgomery, who would later be decorated as an ace for his wartime service. After the war, Mr. Kinnard brought her home to Franklin, and Franklin has never been quite the same. During the 50's and 60's Judge Kinnard devoted her time primarily to rearing not only her own children, Judy, Claiborne and Jon, but also a lot of other children in Franklin. Her farm was the site of many a Scout campout, elementary school Easter egg hunt and BGA tug-of-war.

In 1966, Mr. Kinnard passed away, and by this time the Kinnard children were either grown or almost so. In 1967, Judge Kinnard made a decision which took a lot of her friends by surprise – she enrolled at Vanderbilt Law School. This "career move" was unprecedented at that time for a 47 year old mother of three children. Her farm became the site of yet another regular gathering – her study group of fellow law students, most of whom were in their twenties.

In 1970 Judge Kinnard graduated from Vanderbilt, was admitted to the Bar and began her legal career as an attorney for Commerce Union Bank. Two years later, in 1972, Judge Kinnard was appointed Federal Bankruptcy Judge for the Middle District of Tennessee. With her appointment, Judge Kinnard became the first woman to hold a federal judicial position in the State of Tennessee, and the first woman to serve as a judge on either the state or federal bench in Nashville. In 1972 she was named "Woman of the Year" by the Professional Woman's Club of Davidson County, the only existing professional women's association at that time.

After stepping down from the bench in 1978, Judge Kinnard joined the firm of Chambers and Wiseman. She practiced in that firm until 1989, when she became "of counsel" to the law firm of Stokes & Bartholomew, where she practices today.

Since returning to private practice, Judge Kinnard has been active in Nashville Bar Association and civic affairs. She has served as a director of this Association, and in 1985 was awarded this Bar Association's Pro Bono Award for her dedication in representing indigent individuals. Since the inception of the Pro Bono program, she has represented more Pro Bono clients than any other lawyer in the NBA. Judge Kinnard serves or has served on the boards of the Nashville Symphony, the Cumberland Heights Alcohol & Drug Treatment Center, O'More College, the Vanderbilt Law School Alumni Board, and many others.

When you talk about Judge Kinnard's community involvement, you've got to talk about her unparalleled contributions to Franklin. Most recently, Judge Kinnard served as an Alderman and has served on *the Franklin Board of Zoning Appeals, the Franklin Airport Authority, and the Franklin Charter Study Commission. A founding member and three-time president of the Heritage Foundation of Franklin and Williamson County, she was instrumental in establishing historic zoning in Franklin.*

One of her lesser known endeavors is her effort to introduce New York style living to Franklin. During the last few years she has taken up residence in the second floor townhouse on Main Street in Franklin, directly above several downtown shops.

It is pretty apparent that Judge Kinnard has assumed many different roles in her life:

— a southern belle who married a war hero;

— a loving mother of three children, six grandchildren and at least sixteen godchildren;

— a pioneer among women in the legal profession and the Federal judiciary;

— a dedicated civic and government leader in both Nashville and Franklin."

Throughout all the years, however, if you had to use only one description for Judge Kinnard, the most fitting would be that of a deeply caring and religious person. A long-time Episcopal confirmation instructor, Judge Kinnard attends mass each and every morning, and perhaps as much as any attorney in Nashville, brings her deeply held beliefs to her practice every day. As one of the attorneys at Stokes & Bartholomew said about her, "Mrs. Kinnard transcends generations. She is very compassionate and totally involved with her clients. Judge Kinnard focuses on serving people first and making a living second or third."

On behalf of the Nashville Bar Association, and in recognition of her many contributions to the Nashville legal community, to the cities of Nashville and Franklin, and to the countless people she has helped throughout the years, it gives me great personal pleasure to present the John C. Tune Public Service Award to Judge Ruth Kinnard.

Dudley West

Justin Wilson

On my first day of law school, I asked Ruth what crazy idea had gotten into her son, Wink, with whom I had grown up. I refused to believe her answer that she, not her son, was the student. Then I spent much of the next three years at her home, Martlesham Heath, in Franklin with her, Jim DuBois, Davis Carr, and others who came and went going over our lessons. Years later Davis purchased the Heath.

Ruth was one of the guys. The age differences never came up. She did what we all did both in school and socially. Except she had a certain class, a certain sophistication, and a certain way of understanding what was going on, that put her on a different level. We celebrated each other's accomplishments and shared each other's disappointments. We confided in her and she confided in us. She gave excellent advice, we did not always take. She always kept her confidences. Mainly, we had fun.

We remained friends for the rest of her life and she always remained fun to be around, even in sorrow. Even after she went on the bench, she never lost her love of foolishness or that certain way of understanding with which most of us are not blessed.

Justin P Wilson

Tom Wiseman

Emily and I have many fond memories of Ruth.

One good time was when we went to Chicago for the wedding of Ted Carey and Marnie Huff. I got us lost in a rental car and Ruth could not have been more generous in my frustration.

We had a lovely dinner at her apartment over the store in downtown Franklin with Bill and Debbie Koch and Bill's parents; and Ruth and Emily enjoyed many lunches together at Satsuma.

Family

Jim Faulkner
Ruth's Cousin

MEMORIES OF RUTH KINNARD:

Ruth was not only a close first cousin, but a long-time mentor/advisor and loving friend. In my infancy, she was a caring "sitter" for me, and who incidentally, gave me the nickname "ball-headed butt." Thankfully, I did grow more hair on my head as time passed (wish I had more now).

During my teenage years Ruth lived in Montgomery, Alabama, my hometown, while her sweet, loving and respected husband, Clay, was in Europe leading a squadron of fighter planes that helped defeat the enemy of World War II. It was during this time, the early 40's that she was like a loving sister to me. My family, like many others at that time didn't have much in the way of worldly goods, such as autos; so Ruth would let me drive her fancy Packard convertible – the most eye-catching vehicle of the day! I even used it one Friday night to help transport my football teammates to the game – no buses available because of gas rationing. Needless to say, I didn't allow shoes with cleats to be worn in the car.

In the late 40's, after being discharged from the Navy, and after marrying my sweetheart and life-time mate, Rose, Ruth insisted that I enroll in Vanderbilt University, where she had great influence. During this time, she was my great encourager – resulting in my graduation from Vanderbilt, and on to medical school and my enjoyable career as an Orthopedic surgeon.

Throughout the following years Ruth was and continues to be my loving sister in Christ; but the greatest part of all is knowing that

we will meet again for Eternity in the presence of our loving Lord
and Savior, Jesus Christ.

What memories!!

Jim Faulkner

Carolyn Kinnard Ziffer
Ruth's Cousin

Ruth M. Kinnard was my cousin by marriage who became a soul sister during sixty years of cultivating a deepening relationship through visits, letters and telephone talks.

My first impressions of Ruth were of beauty and sophistication. At a holiday family gathering in the 1940's, with her blonde hair and cigarette in hand, she was the focus of the men's attention as she discussed with them the issues of the time. How pleased I was to be noticed, warmly greeted and complimented by her.

Over the years I could always count on Ruth to be cordially interested in my life, accomplishments and activities. When I chose to marry a man who was "not our kind," Ruth was friendly, encouraging and open; this was of great comfort to me and to my husband. Ruth always expressed love and joy for each child born to us. As they grew, she showed interest in each one, just as she had for me. Whenever our wandering family returned to Franklin, Ruth never failed to invite us to Martlesham Heath for cocktails and catching up on news, or for an afternoon swim in the pool. My husband often remarked, "Ruth is my favorite Kinnard!" By the time our children were in high school, Ruth hosted family dinner parties at Belle Meade Country Club. She was so generous!

As time progressed, many of the clan were claimed by death. Ruth was always present to comfort the bereaved and assist with practical details so the healing could begin. While never at a loss for words, Ruth was sorely challenged when her oldest grandson died in young adulthood.

Ruth loved St. Paul's Church and was methodical, diligent and devout in her prayer life. She was a great comfort to Katrina, a young second cousin, during her terminal illness.

At a young age Ruth's older children addressed their parents directly as "Ruth and Clay." I never thought to ask (because I was only a teenager) if this was suggested and encouraged by the parents, or if the children did it on their own and the parents allowed/accepted it. "How unusual," I thought; my mother insisted upon my calling her "Mother" and my father was to be addressed as "Daddy."

Judge Ruth Kinnard – how proud I was to be her cousin! Many, many times I told of her accomplishments during the 70's and 80's when I was active in the Women's Movement. She was a guiding light, a star.

In later years I remember her wearing a huge pectoral cross, with a Star of David super-imposed. I admired her for this acknowledgement of the roots of Christianity and took it to mean that she wanted to be an open and affirming person while at the same time trusting that her secrets were safe and that she was beloved by her Creator.

I always knew that Ruth was a blessing in my life, but these weeks of meditating on my memories of her have been a bonus blessing.

Postcard from Ruth to Carolyn dated July 1998:
Dear Carolyn,

I hope the reunion went off without a glitch and that you enjoyed it much. It is dreadfully hot here. 95 plus every day and that does not inspire me much. Allison Beasley, who spends every summer in Stonington, Maine, said the weather there is perfect.

Thinking of you so much – with much love. Ruth

Carolyn K. Zipper

John Blue
Ruth's Nephew

I remember Ruth – boy, do I remember Ruth. When she decided something needed to be done, she made sure it happened. And I was the beneficiary on many more than one occasion. The summer of the black T-shirts I remember the best.

I must have been 13 or 14. I'd grown up in West Virginia, not a place where one's attire was taken note of very much, or at least that's the way it seemed to me. For the life of me, I cannot remember what my 13 or 14-year old self was usually dressed in, but whatever it was, I was wearing it when I arrived, with my Mother and siblings, in Franklin to spend some time with the Kinnards.

Whatever I was wearing, it was not what a well-dressed 13 or 14-year old male wore in Middle Tennessee. Ruth immediately spotted that with her laser vision. We'd hardly unpacked the Blue family sedan when Ruth whisked me to Nashville, where I was soon out-fitted with a new casual wardrobe. Khaki chino pants. Stylish leather belt. Oxblood-colored penny loafers. And, most memorably, a couple of black T-shirts.

Jet black they were. Not a hint of decoration on them. Only ominous, heavy black. And did they ever convey a message. What, I didn't know, but I did know, when I wore that outfit, I was conveying a message. It was never clear what studly star of the Grand Old Opry or masculine cowboy of western movie fame I was imitating, but it didn't much matter. I felt like a hunk. Johnny Cash could not have felt more manly.

Not that anyone ever let on that they noticed the fashion statement I was making. Well, Ruth said that I looked nice, but that didn't really count, no matter how grateful I felt. I don't recall any nubile young women throwing themselves at me that summer. But it didn't really matter. I knew that something had changed. The black T-shirts and chinos accompanied me back to West Virginia at the end of the summer. I think I still had the black T-shirts when I went to college years later.

No piece of clothing I've ever since bought has had the same effect on me. I've sometime wondered whether the manufacturer of those T-shirts did more than just dye the material black. Maybe they dipped them in a vat of industrial-strength testosterone?

Julia Blue
Ruth's Niece

Ruth was my aunt, my mother's younger sister, and my memories of her go back many years. During my childhood and teenage years, Mother and my brothers and I visited in Franklin nearly every summer. When we were very young, we called her Tea, the story being that it was a shortened form of "Auntie," which is what Judy, Wink and Jon called our mother. For most of my life, though, she was Ruth. I carry many memories of those visits to Franklin and of Ruth at Martlesham Heath and Willow Plunge. I remember the many things she did to make our visits fun and interesting. Later, during the years Ruth was in law school and I was in veterinary school in Oklahoma, I made many trips from home in West Virginia to Oklahoma. Nashville was the half-way point and Ruth made me welcome each time I came through on my trips back and forth. The last trip from Oklahoma before I settled on the east coast was probably the most memorable. This time, I and a friend were traveling in a huge U-Haul truck, moving the contents of my apartment back east. We were late leaving Oklahoma and the truck was slow; so it was midnight before we pulled into the driveway at Martlesham Heath. Nevertheless, Ruth was out to greet us before we even turned off the lights. We were tired and she was undoubtedly tired, though she would never let you know it. When we opened the back of the truck to get overnight bags, we discovered that my roommate's cat had stowed away in the truck. Ruth was unfazed at the prospect of another guest and made us all comfortable, cat included. After 1980, I saw Ruth only rarely. Actually, I think the next time I saw her was in 1997, when she and Mother and I made a trip to Alabama to visit their cousins. We had such enjoyable conversations on all manner of topics as we drove along. I wish there had been opportunity during my adult life to spend more time in Ruth's company and to have known her more deeply.

Julia Tait Blue

David Blue
Ruth's Nephew

When I was growing up in Romney, West Virginia, we looked forward in the summer time to the day when Mom would say, "Let's get packed up. We're going to Franklin to visit Ruth and Mimi."

That was the highlight of our summer. When we would start on this trip, it would be hot as could be, and, of course, no air conditioning in the car. Mom would be at the wheel. Johnny, Julia and I would be in the car and looking forward to getting to Franklin. Well, at that time, it took us two days. We would drive as far as Kingsport, Tennessee and spend the night. I was delighted to stop there because they had a swimming pool.

We'd get up early the next morning and off to Franklin. Now it was about a four or five hour drive from Knoxville to Franklin, and we just couldn't wait to get there. We always made it about noon time. Ruth and Mimi, my grandmother, and all the family were happy to see us. And from that time on, we were so happy.

Ruth did everything for our pleasure. She would have us all together out at her house and enjoy her swimming pool and then she'd take us places. Every day was a highlight. Jon Kinnard and I were about the same age, and Johnny and Julia and Judy and Wink were too. And all of us together just had a wonderful time.

Now Ruth was a person who went all out for everyone, and when you visited Ruth, you knew you were going to have a great time. Ruth was so patient with all of us. She had a beautiful home and farm and the swimming pool was just delightful. And she always had Mary there in the kitchen. She'd have a lot of young people out there swimming.

When we'd get thirsty, we'd go in the kitchen and Mary would say, "Look in the cupboard and get yourself something to drink. And when I would look in the cupboard, as I told Mom one time, I thought I was looking in the cupboard at Krogers. There was everything good to drink and snacks to eat in that cupboard. Everything at Ruth's home was so relaxed. And everything was at our disposal.

One time, a funny thing I do remember. Ruth was taking Jon and two or three other boys our age somewhere. When we got in the car, the window was down in the back. And one of the boys stuck his head out the window when she let the window up. Ruth didn't realize he had his head stuck out the window. And he started making gurgling sounds. And one of us yelled, "Ruth, wait a minute. His head is stuck out the window." No apparent damage was done.

Ruth was a person who wanted the best for everyone. She took us places, and we had a grand time, but she was always teaching us something. She wanted us to do our best in school. She would encourage us to read. She would talk about what we might want when we went to college and always set good standards ahead for us.

We admired Ruth's abilities in so many ways. And I just looked forward to the times I could be there with her. Of course, with our grandmother, Mimi, there as well it was a special time when we could all be there together, and she made it possible for us to have a wonderful family time.

When our two week vacation was up, I was always disappointed. But when we left, we knew we would be coming back again.

Wink Kinnard
Ruth's Son

Now, the one thing (out of at least 1,000) I recall the most concerns my bad auto accident. I really was on the point of death, for some time primarily because of pneumonia, the "phlegm" in my lungs kept blocking the trachea breathing tube. I could not speak, swallow and barely could make any communication motion. After I was a little better, one of the doctors said he had to be honest with me. One of my two "speaking" cords was crushed as was my larynx. He said I might not be able to speak without the "speaking device." I might not be able to swallow, and other complications.

Mom came in, looked me in the eye and said forcefully, confidently, and calmly that 1) I would be able to speak, 2) I would be able to eat anything I wished, and 3) my recovery would be fast and full. It was as if Mom had just talked to the Lord, and he had instructed her to come and tell me those things. After that I did not doubt my recovery would be complete.

The two things that always impressed me more than anything else was her selflessness and her faith in God. Clay's death really started a time of events that were always "heavy" on her heart. Even with her self confidence it really shook her; they were truly important to each other. It started her "walk with the Lord." One day when Dad was in the bed with cancer Mom went to him and said "she had just found Jesus" but she was 47 years old, to which Dad said "just be glad you're not 67."

About the *Faith in the Lord*, it never left. I would often wonder how she kept from becoming bitter, but the worse things got, the more prayer and faith she would have. Whatever faith I have, I think

it is because of hers. There have been so many times that things have been bad and I could feel myself getting negative and want to ask God – why don't you help. Then I would remember Mom's enormous Faith and I knew that things would get better. But there are things on this earth that are tough; we have no choice but to hang on to the Lord, and He will get us through it.

The second thing I remember is the most simple and I don't really know how to highlight it because it was just a part of her everyday life. She was totally selfless. Whether it was me, you, or an office secretary, she would drop what she was doing in order to help us. It might involve leaving the office for the rest of the day to counsel someone; it might mean she would meet with the couple every week at night. She would do whatever was necessary to help the person with no consideration about how it might inconvenience her or how she felt or any other numerous things. She had a unique gift for making others feel that they were special, had wonderful qualities and were fine individuals. In short they felt good about themselves.

C H Kinnard
d Jnk

Gloria Kinnard
Ruth's Daughter-In-Law

After Ruthie moved from The Heath, when all of the grandchildren were still living at home, she didn't let her city living in downtown Franklin abandon her love of outdoor excursions. One hot June afternoon, while the Cabots were visiting from Boston, all the Kinnards and their offspring were invited to a picnic at the Confederate Cemetery. When we arrived, Mr. Charlie, resplendent in his white uniform, was spreading quilts under the giant cedar tree that guards the cemetery entrance. Several lawn chairs were spaced around in the shade, and baskets bulging with all sorts of intriguing goodies could be seen. Crystal wine glasses of chilled Chardonnay and a choice of lemonade or tea were handed out while the children and adults wandered among the rows of graves, with the adults explaining the significance of the site to the younger children, and especially to the Yankee cousins.

As the sun started to go down, and it became cooler, we gathered on the quilts to enjoy Ruthie's picnic… china plates, complete with silver flatware and linen napkins, which were her signature for her elegant hospitality, were soon filled with Dotson's fried chicken and biscuits and Ruthie's other side dishes. Of course, her special brownies were for dessert, all being Kinnard favorites for many years.

The heat was soon forgotten as we all just luxuriated in being together as a family once again, if not at The Heath, but close to it, sharing memories of it and each other.

Gloria Kinnard

Brandon Kinnard Alexander
Ruth's Granddaughter

My earliest memories of my grandmother Ruthie are of those days spent on her farm, Martlesham Heath, which is now Heath Place subdivision. Swimming, riding horses, playing croquet, and having backyard picnics at her house filled many of my early days.

One of my earliest memories is Ruthie taking Clay and me to see a musical at TPAC in Nashville. Afterwards we spent the night at The Hermitage Hotel. She let us stay up late, order treats from room service after the show and also the next morning for breakfast. After checking out, we went back to the farm with Ruthie.

Another fond memory is eating formal dinners at her house. The table always looked so beautiful with sparkling silver and candles. Clay and I had to be very careful of our table manners because this was of utmost importance to Ruthie, and she always had Mary and Mr. Charlie to help serve us.

Every time I write a thank you note I think of Ruthie and about how she was always writing me notes, even if it were just to thank me for being her granddaughter. She touched my life in so many ways, and has left an everlasting impression on all of us who knew her. She is deeply missed.

Brandon Kinnard Alexander

Edmond Kinnard
Ruth's Grandson

One weekend, when I was around ten years old, Mom and Dad went to an out-of-town wedding, and I was to spend it with Ruthie. Usually I had a sports event to take up Saturdays, but for some reason, this particular Saturday was empty of obligations. To fill the time, Ruth hired me to work for her, and this work was to polish silver. I remember how patiently she explained the process: rub the black with the polish, rinse under the faucet until all the pink is gone, and then dry the piece with the towel. Although the few pieces I saw at the beginning seemed "doable," there seemed to be no end to them as the morning wore on. As fast as one was dried and put away, another appeared.

Just as I was ready to give up and relinquish any profits I may have accrued, she announced that we were finished, and that I had performed excellently. Ruthie then gave me thirty dollars for the two hours I worked for her. I felt like I was rich! And most importantly, I knew from then on that if I worked, I could get money!

Edmond Kinnard

Jon Kinnard
Ruth's Son

Growing up, I remember the drive home going out Lewisburg Pike, turning toward the Confederate Cemetery that took us to our driveway. I didn't realize it, but by today's standards, we had some land then. On it was a spot my mother called the "Cedar Grove." This implies a forest of cedars which it wasn't. There were about five trees, not that big, but close enough to make you feel as if you were in a forest. At least as a child, it felt like a forest, one that you knew and one that protected you. It was in this spot my mother always took me when she felt I had something on my mind that needed talking about. The "Grove" was not far from the back door of the house. Usually it would be late in the afternoon when we strolled down the hill, and we'd go to our place to sit and talk. She would always start the conversation with a laugh or a hug and eventually I would spill my worries on her. She never had to think more than a second before coming up with a solution to the problem. And almost always it could be solved by taking action.

Unfortunately, taking action has never been one of my strong points. Consequently she often had to think of a way to motivate me.

My memories of the numerous hurdles while growing up are vague, but there is one that stands out. I had started kindergarten. This was a new frontier for me. Up to this point my world consisted of Ma, Mr. Clay, Tia, Wink May and Mr. Charlie. Now there was a new port on my horizon: a mob of little children.

An important reason for going to Ms. Inga's was Allison Holland, my first crush. Her curly blonde hair and big smile caught the eye of other boys too. There was one in particular who knew much more about the ways of the world than I did. I'm not sure I was in the running for her affection, but my streetwise classmate wanted no competition. The result was that he asked me if I wanted to fight, and my answer was not yes.

This predicament led Ma and me to the "Cedar Grove" one afternoon after kindergarten. I confessed my feelings for Allison Holland and the confrontation with my rival for her affection. Her moment of thought was longer than normal, but the answer that came out was the usual remedy of action. She said, "I will pay you 50 cents for every time you get in a fight." I am sure this put a frown, not a smile, on my face. And I don't remember ever getting 50 cents out of the deal. As a matter of fact, it wasn't until an incident that happened in the second grade that I could have collected, but by then the deal had been forgotten and replaced with other hurdles to be crossed.

The memories of Ma are so many. One recent one:

Ma was in her late seventies. She was still going to the office, but her law practice was not as demanding as it once was by choice. Even though her job was requiring less time, I can't remember a time when she did not have a goal to accomplish.

For several years, one of her goals was to make peppermint wreaths for Christmas gifts. She had moved from her apartment on Main Street to the small house on "Evans Alley" as she insisted on called it. I remember that in November and December when I would stop by, she would be sitting on the sofa with florist wire in one hand and red and white peppermints in the other, carefully stringing the candy around a coat hanger formed in a small circle. All around her would be strands of red and green ribbon waiting placement on the finished products.

My small part in all of this, since I had the pliers and wire cutters, was to supply the round coat hanger wreath forms. One night she called me pretty late and asked if I had anymore of the forms made. I said no, but that I would make some more that week. Ma then asked me (with a little more Montgomery, Alabama tone than usual) if I could possibly make three more and bring them over. As my father always said, "Ruth never puts off until today what she could have done day before yesterday." I said yes, and then hung the phone up a little more abruptly than usual, but then went on to make the requested wreath hangers. I then took them over as requested. I knocked on the door. I opened the door and was greeted by the usual cloud of smoke. She was on the sofa working away on the wreaths and smiling at me. "Oh thank you, dahling," she gratefully said. At that moment I realized that Ma had done not just things like this, but much more than this, every day of my life.

Many memories in between, but the most important of all, the one that stays with me always, is knowing that my mother loved me and would do anything to help me.

Laura Kinnard
Ruth's Daughter-In-Law

When I learned of the plan to compose a book consolidating stories and remembrances of my mother-in-law and friend, Ruth Kinnard, I was thrilled. I felt honored to be asked to make a contribution. I do not know if I have a 'favorite story' even though I have been in the family for 20 years now. So I decided that I would focus on a dimension of her that comes to my mind easily when I think of her and our last years together.

The year Campbell entered Kindergarten, Ruthie asked Jon and me if she could pick him up from school three days a week. The kindergarten program ended each day at noon. We appreciated her offer and accepted. She seemed thrilled with the prospect and it would allow them some special time together. And with this my story begins.

Now little did we know that when Campbell started his school career, he not only started Kindergarten, but he was enrolled in 'The Saffron Walden School'. While not a formal educational institution, it is one I would gladly recommend if it was still in existence today. You might say it was a specialized learning environment led by Ruthie herself.

At Saffron Walden School, Campbell learned many things. First he learned how to save, spend and tithe. He learned how to write a check, tell time and negotiate contracts. He learned the art of polishing silver, making peanut brittle and making Christmas crafts. He went to the Police Department and County Courts to observe and learn about the law and judicial processes. He went to the Fire Department. He learned the proper way to set a table, which may explain how he won a table setting contest his first year of Jr. Cotillion. Then there was the lesson of persistence…never give up…as they traveled about Franklin and Nashville searching for the latest action figures for Star Wars or Beanie Babies or even a sale on nutcrackers. Campbell started two of his favorite hobbies during this time…coin collecting and stamp collecting. The results of this training go on and on.

Now all these things may seem rather daunting for a 5 year old. But Ruthie quite often gave someone tasks that were slightly beyond their capabilities and displayed a confidence in others that was enabling and encouraging. "Mr. Clay always said you should pay someone a little more than they think they are worth," she would say. And that is how I remember her, always a mentor, a giver and supporter of others.

Laura Kennard.

Campbell Kinnard
Ruth's Grandson

DAR

Dar, my Grandmother, can most accurately be described as my best teacher. She valued learning and prized success (particularly because that is all she would accept). She would pick me up from school most days at 3:10 pm sharp to take me to her house or, as she called it, B and R (Baskin Robbins) for ice cream. Whether we went home or to get ice cream I always ended up learning something new. The most frequent and repetitive learning experience was going to the bank. At the bank I either wrote checks or she explained to me about how money worked.

When I was younger she introduced me to the "Saffron Walden School." She taught me basic skills such as: counting money, telling time on a clock, and about God and the Church. I can still remember her drilling me on telling time and counting money. This helped me value learning at a young age and to always do better than your best.

Dar was not only my greatest teacher, but also the loving grandmother that put everybody else ahead of herself and spoiled everyone.

Campbell Kinnard

Chris Cabot
Ruth's Son-In-Law

Dear Ruth,

When was it that we first made our compact? It was always unspoken and, thus, hard for me to pinpoint in time. It was also subtle and so one-sided in my favor that I didn't realize it. Eventually I caught on, and I knew that you knew that I knew that we had a deal.

It began sometime in the summer of 1974, as so many of your friendships, with an invitation to The Heath.

"Chris Cabot! Come out to The Heath for the 4th of July. We're having a few people over. Simple supper. Hot weather. Swimming pool. Oh, and Tia will be home for the weekend."

TIA! – my pulse rose. Invitation accepted.

I had first laid eyes on Judy Kinnard at the Steeplechase that May. I had stopped by the Steeplechase on my way into Nashville to work at The Associated Press (my hours were crazy) and in the 15 minutes I was there I saw the most beautiful woman I will ever see, your daughter. The photo of Tia in her rain hat that my friend, Alex Steele, took that day still stands on my bureau. Of course, it was at your suggestion in the first place that I had stopped by. They were your box seats.

The 4th of July at the Heath went just fine; I did not disgrace myself. Did I ever tell you that I rode my bike out to The Heath that weekend not for the exercise, but so that I wouldn't have a car, thinking cleverly that nobody would want to drive me home? So I got to sleep over on the sofa in the sitting room and, more to the point, have breakfast with you and Tia the next morning. Later, we tossed my bike into the back of the old El Camino and Mr. Charlie drove me home.

You picked up the pace pretty quickly though. Remember in September bringing Tia to my place in Brentwood (I just happened to be on your way home from picking her up at the airport)? Our compact, which was new if it even then existed (I think it did), did not require too much of me – some whiskey and a little cooking. My signal culinary success that evening was to serve the salad after the main course, as did my mother and "as they do in France." When you said, approvingly, that was how it was done in South Alabama, I felt my prospects rise.

Soon came another invitation to The Heath, when my parents were down in October. Tia, again, just happened to be home from Philadelphia for that weekend. Wasn't it grand when my father saw the portrait of Mr. Clay in the library and said "I've seen that man before, who is he?" It turned out that both men had been in the Eighth Air Force in England in WW II.

You know, my romantic old man figured it out right then and there. Later that evening back at their hotel, he told Mom that "Chris is going to marry that girl." "Don't be ridiculous, he hardly knows her," she replied. They were both right. Even the "ridiculous" part. Objectively, in 1974 my chances of getting Judy Kinnard even to go out on a date with me, let alone marry me, were, indeed, ridiculous.

But you took care of that, Ruth, in short order, didn't you? You asked me back out to The Heath for Christmas. You dropped out, suddenly, from the group trip to Martinique, leaving Tia and me to our own devices, with brother Jon as indulgent chaperone. That was New Years weekend of 1975. We were married in May.

Only later, at a reflective moment on our honeymoon in Mexico did it come to me that perhaps Tia and I were not the only architects of our great good fortune. I clearly remember watching Tia cross a stone courtyard and saying to myself, almost aloud, "Ruth, you did this whole thing, didn't you?" (I can be slower on the uptake than I like to admit.)

Thenceforth, it became my task to understand and perform my part of our deal.

I thought I did OK the night Heath was born. Jon and I snuck you down the fire exit of Parkview Hospital (minor surgery), whisked you across the parking lot to the maternity floor of Baptist, and into the waiting room to smoke cigarettes with us. You were a fugitive in sunglasses at midnight, and you were there when Heath was born. Tia says I should have been helping her do the Lamaze breathing technique and not out committing misdemeanors with you and Jon.

And what about after several years of marriage when I finally was "allowed" to smell the honeysuckle on the Lane, a smell you always had insisted was "too sweet for a Yankee to smell?"

Seriously, though, my side of our compact was simple: to try to be the best husband, man and father I could be. The terms of this obligation were not explicit demands or requirements. You never would do that. Rather, my part of our deal was to try to meet standards of excellence, quality, character and behavior that I felt I should to be worthy of your daughter and granddaughters and to be a part of your family. I'm still trying, and thankful every day for the chance you gave me to do so.

God bless you.

Chris Cobor

Judith Kinnard Cabot
Ruth's Duaghter

Slender chicken sandwiches, tomatoes glued to their rounds of Sunbeam with dollops of Hellman's, pimento cheese triangles on a silver tray. Melon balls, strawberries and grapes mounded a foot high on another. And tiny chess pies piled into a pyramid on another huge tray lined with a paper doily to sop up the butter oozing from the crust. And there are almond crescent cookies and miniature peach turnovers sprinkled with confectioners sugar. Huge gallon screw top jars filled with fruit tea ready to be poured into silver pitchers.

May May took hours, never to be rushed, to prepare.

This is how we lived, with an overflowing generosity set by our mother who presided over the terrace or the expansive rooms inside at all hours and in all seasons. Often we took such delectables to the Confederate Cemetery to sit amid the rows of chunky headstones of long dead southern soldiers on incongruously gay tablecloths. Sometimes we went to Willow Plunge where the pavilion added open air excitement with screened protection from the bugs. The concrete floor cool and smooth on a hot summer night. The tin roof exploding with raindrops or even hail. And the air, when it moved, as before a storm, would bring the perfume of honeysuckle on the lane. Outside, the lure of fireflies by night and Junebugs by day that every Franklin child remembers from summer days.

Our life was magic, made magic by our mother. And the Heath, though not her only home, was her perfect stage when we were still all together.

In early spring, an overcoat, pumps, a scarf around her head, and large glasses often wreathed in smoke, she would ride the lawnmower to get an early start on the manicuring of the fifty acres she considered lawn. Once Mr. Charlie came to do that, she might be riding a go cart with Jon, or later with a grandchild, filling the soft air with a laugh that revealed the glorious co-ed she had been and still was at heart.

Her memory of those days as a young woman right out of college when she became traveling secretary to Tri Delta, came to me in a letter written when she was still gripped with grief over my father's death a year earlier.

25 August, '67

Dearest Tia,

It is raining – and a tired, sad, day – your opinion to the contrary! And tired sad days make me tired and sad and also make me remember the tired sad thirties when we were young and concerned with "security" and avoidance of failure to the degree that answers weren't important as they seem to be to you who are young in the sixties – or to those of us who have gotten to be fifty in the sixties.

But you are going to Chicago today – that is a wonderful town – and we never got to talk about it or the memories – mine – of Chicago and the Mid West.

So, my darling daughter, these words are:

1) To fill a sad tired day for me

2) To tell you briefly a memory

When I went to Chicago, believe me, I should have been impressed! A plantation in the black belt of Alabama, a childhood in Montgomery, and a few golden years at a state university would have conditioned me that way. But I wasn't impressed – except with the excitement of a city – because Chicago is a friendly town. And I felt at home. It's hard to explain, and I loved the anonymity of lots of people – something I had never known before.

By the time I arrived in Chicago, Baby Face Nelson had already seen his last movie, and prohibition had been repealed, and the banks had closed and reopened, and there was the WPA and artists and writers were eating again – regularly though not well – and they were painting murals on government buildings instead of starving in garrets.

And there was war in the air, we knew. Not the glamour of WWI, but a recklessness because even though there were America First advocates, everyone knew that it was a matter of time before we were involved – actively.

So I had what must have been a tired sad room at the YWCA. The saving grace must have been that it was on the near North Side and I could wander. Wandering when one is 22 is almost an essential thing – and I had lots of time for that. And I saw Elliot Nugent in "The Male Animal" and whatever other play that had a two week run in Chicago.

I spent Sundays at the Art Institute and considered myself highly intellectual and salved my uncreative nature by believing that there was a real need for people like me – to appreciate the creative ones. And I walked for hours along the lake shore. I rode the elevated trains and was – in truth – in love with the people and the world and being alive – and on an elevated train. And I read pages and pages of Thomas Wolfe and mooned about his words.

It was, in fact, like the butterfly wings of Scott Fitzgerald that Hemingway talks about. How sad – it is a truth – that the wings of a butterfly are always bruised by time and circumstance. Or at least the wings of those who are vulnerable, less confident, less, even, courageous than a Hemingway.

But all of these are memories of youth. They happen to be mine, but they are the same for ever so many of us.

My places in Chicago – and I saw them all I think – are as real today and every lovely moment is rather more than lovely in retrospect.

The Medinah Club on North Michigan had been taken over by the Navy, and it was there that my K.A. beau from Alabama was stationed. There was the Palmer House and Eddy Duchin at a piano and naval uniforms overfilling the room. And a small Italian restaurant, Ricardos, under an el which served green noodles in such an atmosphere. I believed I was an "expatriate" on the Left Bank. And State Street and the "joints" – actually they were – which I had known about, and which were gay and "forbidden fruit" to coin a phrase. But the Pump Room at the Ambassador East on Sunday morning for breakfast was the farthest spot from Alabama, and I loved its elegance – or what I thought was elegance – best of all.

The Black Hawk Restaurant was a dancing spot and late night radio programs – remotes you would call them – originated there. The Wayne King music and the blue lights made it wondrous then.

And shop-window looking in the Loop was the way we ended the night and I am quite sure that I saw emeralds as big as the Ritz in Peacock's – is that the name – displays. And we must have seen in an old movie about getting a bottle of milk from the delivery truck and sitting on the curb to drink it – because we did that too. It was very gay and very unreal and very young.

None of us smoked pot or drank much whiskey (we were intoxicated enough with youth). Nor did we know it was chic to drink wine at dinner. We did have long and earnest conversations about Hitler and the Jews and we wanted to right that wrong. And we made choices between Fascism and Communism and vowed we would have joined one of "the groups" but we never had the courage.

Isn't it strange that my K.A. beau is now the Suffragan Bishop of Alabama, and he's probably so inundated with tired sad people and tired sad clergy that he never thinks of that year of 1940 when we created a brave new world in Chicago.

And I wouldn't have thought of it either if it hadn't been for your weekend. But that's what you get for having a sentimental parent. Have a good weekend. Going to Chicago won't be a Babylon Revisited for you, but it can be good to discover a new city when one is young.

 I love you much,
 Ma

She laughed at herself. "I'm very discriminating in my friendships," she often said. "I love anyone who says 'Hello, Mrs. Kinnard'." And for her those relationships were everything.

The next time we see each other I'll tell you, if you'll let me, whatever answers or questions I've learned in these brief years I've known. They aren't many. I believe I do know, however, that happiness means a moment (or moments) now and then; that life, for the most part, is swimming upstream; that nobody did promise me a rose garden; that relationships, in the final analysis, are the basis of those moments (not professional satisfaction); that from Faulkner, the real victory in life is to survive.

I do know that there is a moment when each of us grows up. And there is a moment when each of us grows old. Now I know both of these moments, and that means another reassessment. I'm capable of that.

The strength of her, the seeming certainty of her life made me know that I should find a way to grow on my own. So I chose California, or rather it chose me with a job offer. Even that far away, she could tell when I needed help. And her support was constant.

I've known that perhaps you were going through another period of personal growth. Painful though it is, it is essential.

Further, it is the reason none of us (even though some may give a different impression) ever gets it together for always. Life itself, if it means anything, is change and demands flexibility, growing periods, and then we have a respite until time for the next evaluation.

No one, no one, is secure until he comes to terms with his religious belief. The only security is belief in Him and faith in Him.

But this too comes and goes. During the last six months of Clay's illness and the year thereafter, my faith and belief were strong.

I still believe, and I still have faith as long as I say my prayers. But lately I have not been so faithful as to observe the discipline.

All the transcendental meditation movement is nothing more than what Jesus recommended 2000 years ago. Because prayer is meditation.

As for finding the answers, human beings are limited. The answers come through prayer for wisdom and help (Grace) from the Holy Spirit. Belief in Jesus is a gift from God. You cannot work for the initial gift. You simply ask Him to give you the gift of belief. You get the gift of belief when you are ready to accept it.

And

Once you get the gift, you nurture it by daily prayers and by asking Him to show you the way, the truth, the path for you.

I keep denying what he tells me. I want – being human – what I want. When all he has ever told me is to show his love to the people he

193

puts in my path.

Sometimes I am tired of showing His love. But it is what he asks me to do. And if I would submit and do it with joy, then he gives me the strength and courage to do it easily.

What I am trying to say is that none of us has the strength within ourselves. It only comes from Him.

He doesn't promise us a life free from pain and hurt, even agony. That is not in the scheme of life. He knew that best of all. But He does promise us Grace (help) and He makes good that promise.

All of this is hasty, but it is from the heart. You are right. I cannot help you. You cannot help me except by showing love to each other.

Her capacity for love and support seemed boundless to me. My stamina often fell short and nothing could be so wonderful as a weekend of R and R at the Heath in the nest I had fled.

On one such visit, she picked me up at the airport with a rather sly smile. Anticipating a short drive to my old room, with a marble bath – I hadn't lived in such luxury since I left – she announced that we would have to stop by to check on a new young friend who had been in an automobile accident. He had a concussion and no one to look after him.

I sank into irritation, if not gloom. Oh no, another acolyte. She chatted the whole ride, ignoring my mood. He had written a story about her for the Associated Press when she was named the first woman in Tennessee to be appointed to the Federal Bench. He had made all his own furniture in a charming farmhouse near Moran Road. He had a belt buckle from a Union Soldier. What! She got my attention. A Yankee belt buckle!

We veered off Hillsboro Road, up a hill to the small farmhouse. Inside, on a sofa he made, with a bandage on his head, lay the patient.

It was Chris Cabot. Though I had met him before, Ruthie's plot was full blown by now. He cooked for us – hamburgers filled with tiny bits of onion. Hours later we left.

Months later we were married. We had several blissful years in the "Little House" at the Heath where our first daughter, Heath, was born. As an aside: Chris' father often remarked that he was so happy that "Col. Kinnard had not been stationed at Claxton Gibbet!"

After our move to Boston, she came often to visit. On one trip she had an interview at the Episcopal Divinity School in Cambridge. She was not able to get the necessary recommendation from the Bishop of Tennessee to complete her application as women in the clergy were still a rarity. So, refusing to be stopped by this disappointment, she simply turned her life into a personal vocation, free from the bounds of the church, to fulfill her life's work.

It is startling to me to remember that she was only married for twenty three years. Those years seemed to me to be the core of her life. All that came before was preparation for her marriage to my father. And all that came after, however brilliant her accomplishments, was marking time.

In the South, many men put their wives on a pedestal. In our family, it was quite the opposite. As an example: My father's commute, from the front of the farm, where Franklin Concrete was, to the middle of the farm, where our house was, took about five minutes, certainly at the speed he drove. My mother said that he needed time to decompress when he got home, since he didn't have the luxury of a proper commute. So we were not allowed to speak to him for an hour after his return.

After my father's death, the autumn after I graduated from college, I know she would say to each of us that she was only marking time.

Dearest Tia,

The loneliness you expressed is what every human being feels so desperately so it's good to give in every now and again, and then try to cope again.

I never knew anything but loneliness, except those years I had Clay. Now I have it again. But that, darling child, is the human condition.

In the end, the story of my mother, more than anything else, is a love story.

Judith Kinnard Cabot

195

Heath Cabot
Ruth's Granddaughter

For much of my childhood, Ruthie, or "Dar" as she was named by the toddler I once was (an infantile mimesis of her cooes of "darling"), stood for everything that was good and proper – and in some ways, quite intimidating. It was she who needled my back with the tips of her fingers to improve my posture, who scolded me about which fork to use, who insisted that I get confirmed, despite my scowling and the burgeoning existential crises of my preteen years. Elegant, grand, and always expansively loved by everyone – for years I was a little (and sometimes more than a little) scared of her. But when I look back, it's amazing it took me so long to realize that she was also, quite simply, incredibly cool. Here are a couple of snapshots, vignettes, of her imminent coolness, which always make me smile.

The Toothfairy

The summer after I was in kindergarten, we visited Dar for a couple of weeks, as we did every summer. But it was also the first summer after she sold the Heath (my namesake as well as my birth-place). She had moved into a beautiful apartment in downtown Franklin, which was clean, modern, and bright, but which was, nonetheless, simply not the same. It was incredibly hot and humid, as always. And while in the past we could always just step outside to the turquoise pool, here there was no pool, and no acres upon acres of quiet bluegrass; instead, the hot pavement of Fourth Avenue North and Main Street awaited us. So I stayed mostly in the air-conditioning, listening and dancing to Michael Jackson's "Thriller" on the tape-recorder. Like all the other little kids, I was obsessed with him (wouldn't he have loved that!).

One day my cousins asked me to come to the Carnton Club to swim, an extremely welcome invitation. I was quite the water bug at the time, as was my cousin Brandon, and we were having a great time diving and playing in the chlorine. But one of my two front teeth was very loose, not quite ready to come out, and when one of the lifeguards saw me displaying it, he told me that I was not allowed to dive, in case I were to choke on it. I asked him: if I were to lose it, could I dive again, and he said "sure." So I knocked it out on one of the concrete lips of the pool, wrapped it in tissue, and stowed it away in the pocket of my shorts; then went on with my water-games. When I got back to Dar's, I boasted of my brave evasion of the lifeguard's rules, displaying my tooth proudly. For safe-keeping, I put the precious tooth in one of Dar's often-used tooth-white ash-trays, anticipating the toothfairy's visit that night. Later, when I came looking for it to put in under my pillow, I was surprised and tearful to find that Dar had, (unknowingly and understandably of course), thrown it out while emptying the ash-tray. So I went to bed sulkily, with no tooth for the toothfairy.

When I woke up the next morning, I felt under my pillow to see if the toothfairy had come anyway, but to no avail. Then I heard Dar calling my name, saying "Heath – come look!" So I went sadly, still sulking, downstairs to the living room. And what to my wondering eyes should appear but an assortment of Michael Jackson items spread out on the sofa, including a glossy book of photographs and a picture-disc of "Thriller." I met Dar's big look of surprise with happy squealing. Then the phone rang, and Dar told me to answer it. On the other end of the line I heard a musical voice say: "Good morning, Heath. This is the toothfairy. Did you find my gifts?"

"Yes, toothfairy!"

"I felt so bad that your grandmother threw out your tooth that I brought you extra gifts."

"Thank you, toothfairy!"

"Be good, Heath. Goodbye, goodbye" (musical voice softly fading out)

Happily, I spent the rest of the day marveling at my luck and my new Michael Jackson paraphernalia. The experience made such an impression on me that when I returned to school in the fall, I wrote a piece about it that was published in the school newspaper – I wanted so much to brag of my encounter with the toothfairy.

Later, when I conned my mother into telling me, "truthfully," whether the toothfairy "really" existed, I asked her "what about that time at Dar's?" She told me that Dar had gotten up early and bought the Michael Jackson items for me, and asked an actress friend to call as the toothfairy. It remains one of my most joyful memories, and it is then that I began to get a hint of how cool Dar really was: all of my friends coveted my Michael Jackson book, and the picture-disc is a collector's item!

San Francisco, and Leopard-Print Bra-straps

In 1997, my first year in college, Edie Caldwell invited Dar to San Francisco for a visit, which was officially organized around hearing the Buddhist scholar Robert Thurman speak at the San Francisco Zen Center. I, who had spent a lovely few days at a Buddhist conference with Edie, and who was much in need of a visit with Dar, decided to meet her there. We spent a wonderful, stimulating weekend in San Francisco (where I had never been but, later, moved), surrounded by Edie and her artist friends.

But one of those days, I also made a date to meet up with a friend of mine who, in high school at least, was the epitome of cool. A couple of years older than me, Amy is a beautiful, well-endowed, "exotic," feminist, "experimental," sexually fluid type who at the time was studying electronic art and film at Mills College. She also, at the time, tended to be extremely scantily clad, usually dressed in various overly-stretched, torn, or slinky fabrics. Amy also made a habit of asking shocking, personal, private questions of people she had just met. In short, she was not necessarily someone whom I wanted my elegant, proper (though certainly fun) grandmother to spend a lot of time with. Nonetheless, Dar insisted I have her come to the Union Square hotel where we were staying and have breakfast with us.

True to form, Amy arrived in torn black jeans and a too-small black tank-top displaying enormous, shiny, leopard-print bra straps. Sitting down to breakfast, she immediately took her jacket off and, basically, propped her rack on the table. But polite and warm as always, Dar engaged her in conversation, saying, "Now, Amy, tell me about you." An hour and a half later, they were fast friends, having covered the terrains of radical feminism and legal activism. As we got up from the table, and Amy and I prepared to head out for a couple of hours, Dar said, "Now, Amy, I have to tell you: I just LOVE your bra!"

Elizabeth Cabot
Ruth's Granddaughter

Ruthie, who, to my sister and me will always be remembered as Dar, possessed that rare, magnetic ability to draw a person in. When she entered a room, she appeared as if she was an aging movie star, elegantly clothed in her uniform of big, dark, oh-so-glamorous Audrey Hepburn-esque sunglasses, enormous gold-linked cross and smaller, more delicate one, suit skirt and silk blouse, stockings and Ferragamo heels. In her later years, she carried a silver-topped cane that imbued the Southern lady with a debonair, rakish charm, as if she might at any moment break into some wild rendition of a razzle-dazzle Gene Kelly dance number.

My sister, Heath, has written of how eminently cool Dar was, and to this, I will add my own vignette. At seventeen, I was still very much unsure in my own skin; I had chopped off my hair (hoping to look like some waifish French gamine), but this only exacerbated my feelings of insecurity. I felt that I looked, at best, gender ambiguous and, at worst, like a preteen boy. I had also gotten a tattoo on my lower back which read "strength" in Chinese. My parents were incredibly gracious about my hair fiasco, but remained conspicuously reticent on the subject of the tattoo. (In an attempt to soften the blow, I had said that the tattoo was of the henna variety, and thus semi permanent. However, when it failed to fade after three months, the truth began to dawn on them). When visiting Dar over the summer, the subject of my tattoo invariably came up, as she had no doubt been briefed by my mother. Although I was unsure as to what her response would be, I confess that I was taken aback when she exclaimed, in her husky drawl and bearing a wry smile: "If I were

201

younger, I expect I might get a tattoo. Perhaps I still will!"

Although I am fairly certain that Dar would never have dreamed of tattooing herself, her acceptance of my choice (albeit one I now regret) was a remarkably modern reaction, coming from someone who had long stood, in my mind, as the beacon of traditional elegance and proper comportment. I had long been familiar with the persona of my grandmother as an altruistic healer of sorts – a woman to whom so many would flock, seeking comfort and sage advice. However, my sister and I were always intimidated by the standard to which we felt she held us up (and to which, we feared, we paled in comparison). I now realize that much of this was our own projection; our own insecurities rather than her judgment.

I know this because Dar and I truly became close companions, confidants and partners in crime during a particularly difficult period in my young life, when she saw that I was lost and in need of help, and reached out to me, as I am sure she did to many of you. The relationship that I was blessed to have with Dar in her last years changed my life, when she became so much more than my grandmother; she became my closest friend.

Elizabeth Cabot

Photo by Elizabeth Cabot